MY JOURNEY

© GIL TODACHINE

by Jo Ann Craver

ISBN: 978-0-9840680-3-6

iBookPublishing Company
Overland Park, Kansas

A Few Words of Thanks From My Grateful Heart—

To Ruth Walker, whose friendship and encouragement has blessed me through the years. In this instance, her editing assistance was invaluable—among other things—she helped me sort out the commas! Also to Betty Murray, who made some excellent suggestions. And to dear Kathy Bowersock, her computer skills helped make this book possible. I "couldna' done it" without you girls! God bless you, each one!

Thanks also to Gil Todachine for use of his picture on the front cover. If you are interested in Gil's artwork, you may contact him at:

Gil Todachine Design

P O Box 4119

Kayenta AZ 86033

(928) 658-3214

mediatech77@yahoo.com

gil_todachine@hotmail.com

My Introduction
To Apache Land

A wickiup—1967

I was totally unprepared for the sight that met my eyes when
I looked out the window that cold January morning in 1967. I
didn't see any "real houses," only a few small buildings and many
other strange structures. Seeing my puzzled look, the missionary pastor Brother Knotts quietly explained, "The people live in
those, they are called wickiups. They build them by tying poles
together at the top, leaving a space for the smoke to come out, as
they have a small fire on the dirt floor inside. They thatch them
with heavy grass, then put pieces of canvas around the outside to
help keep the cold out and the heat in." I noticed that each one
had a small entrance way where the door was located. Near each
wickiup there was a structure of poles with a brush roof—no
walls. Later I learned they called these a *shade* or a *ramada*.

It gets cold in this part of Arizona because of the high elevation. On that cold morning I saw women outside in long dresses,

each one with a blanket wrapped around her shoulders. Later I learned they call this type of dress a camp dress— the traditional dress for an Apache woman. Since they called the place they lived their "camp," these were camp dresses. I looked in disbelief at those women, in their long dresses and blankets, outside on that cold January morning—cooking over open fires.

I was stunned, to say the least. I felt as if I had awakened in another time and another place. This feeling intensified when I met the people and heard them speaking a different language. That day I experienced "culture shock," although it was years before I heard the term.

I am happy to say that in the years that have passed, modern housing has come to all the reservations. However, many Apache women still wear their camp dresses and many Apaches still speak their language. The same can be said for other tribes that continue to hold onto their culture and language

How I Got There

Looking back, it's difficult to pinpoint an exact starting place for the turns and twists that set me on a certain path. Many things worked into the pattern of my life leading to the day I got on a Greyhound Bus in Oshkosh, Wisconsin, and headed West.

That day there was one thing I knew for sure; the Lord was leading me. I had heard His still small voice in my innermost being, telling me to go to Arizona and help Olan Knotts and his wife with their missionary service to American Indians.

The Knotts were "retired" ministers who felt called to go to Arizona and do whatever they could to minister to American Indians. About a year before I got on that bus, I heard them speak in my home church in Mount Morris, Pennsylvania. After the service, Brother Knotts gave me an invitation to "come out and help them." I tried to shrug it off— but the voice of the Lord echoed in that invitation.

My adventure began that January day in 1967, when I got off
the Greyhound Bus in Globe, Arizona. Globe is about 60 miles
from where the Knotts lived. They were serving as missionary
pastors among the White Mountain Apaches in a remote village
called Cibecue, located on the Fort Apache Reservation.

It was late afternoon when Brother Knotts picked me up at the bus
station. We headed north on Highway 60 through the magnificent
Salt River Canyon—but I was too tired to enjoy the view. In the years
to come I would drive the five miles of switch-back curves down one
side of this canyon, across the mighty Salt River, then drive the five
miles of similar curves up the other side to the top—hundreds of
times. That day I didn't even have a driver's license.

By the time we reached the turn-off to Cibecue, deep utter
darkness enveloped us. Brother Knotts said it would be another
14 miles to the village, about half of it gravel. As we bumped and
jostled along, I began to wonder if we would ever get to the end
of that rough road. Finally, we turned through an open gate between strands of barbed wire and crossed a cattle guard, the first
one I had ever seen. We stopped in front of the little house the
Knotts called home, it was right by the church. Dear Sister Knotts
had a warm meal ready. I remember eating a little and stumbling
off to bed.

After my initial shock, I slowly began to fit into the flow of life
on the reservation. I helped Brother Knotts by starting a children's
church and teaching Sunday School. I went with the women
"camp calling." We would go bouncing along the unpaved roads,
usually in the back of a pickup truck, to camps beyond the village.
The ladies would sing in Apache and I soon learned enough to
join in. Then they would take turns talking (not preaching) to the
people where we stopped. When it was my turn, they would interpret what I said into Apache.

Later I learned enough Apache to basically understand what
people were saying and could even speak a little. However, my
Apache friends got lots of laughs out of my efforts. In fact, laugh-

ter plays a major part in the lives of Native Americans. Once you get to know them, you realize the idea of the stoic Indian is far from true. The first 11 years of my journey were spent among the Apaches. Many of the stories in this book depict people and scenes from those years.

About six months after my arrival, Brother Knotts suffered a heart attack and went to be with the Lord. I stayed on in Cibecue for another six months, assisting the missionaries who came to take over the work.

Sells And San Carlos

Then, I got hepatitis from a sweet little Apache child that I carried into the church. The poor little thing was trying to walk, hanging onto her mother's camp dress, as her mother had her hands full with a crying baby. She told me that she had taken her little girl to White-river to the government run Indian hospital— they told her there was nothing wrong with her—they just gave her some baby aspirin. Later we found out the child was in the hospital with hepatitis—and shortly afterwards I found out that I, too, had hepatitis!

I spent 10 days in the small hospital in Show Low—and I mean small—it only had 10 beds. They put me in a makeshift room, as I had to be isolated. Today, Show Low has a large modern hospital. My bill for those 10 days was a little over $300! How times have changed! However, paying that bill took almost every penny I had.

When I got out of the hospital I went to Sells on the Papago (now called Tohono O'odham) Reservation to recuperate. I stayed with Rodger and Esther Cree, the missionaries in Sells. At the time I was not well-acquainted with the Crees. However, some years earlier my brother had been a blessing to them when they were itinerating in Pennsylvania. So, when the Crees heard of my illness, they invited me to stay with them after I got out of the hospital. Brother Cree borrowed a motor home (I was too weak to sit up for the long ride to Sells) and drove several hundred miles to get me.

In a few months I was feeling better, and had even renewed my driving skills. I had learned to drive in high school—years before, but did not have a driver's license. Almeda, the young woman who was working with the Crees let me use her car, and I got my first Arizona drivers license! But I didn't get a car until I went back to Pennsylvania that summer. I was invited to speak in several churches, and so the Lord provided enough for a down payment on my first car—a white Ford Falcon!

Another important part of my journey happened while I was in Sells—I received my Home Missions appointment. I had applied for and received my license to preach while I was in Cibecue, so was eligible to apply for appointment. Later I completed the Berean School of the Bible courses and was ordained.

In those days no one asked if you had any financial support. A pastor from West Virginia, Robert Smith, who was in Cibecue when Brother Knotts died from the heart attack, took it upon himself when he returned home, to raise some support for me. Would you believe that 43 years later, some of those churches that Brother Smith asked to support me are still doing so. Now, that's being faithful!

From Sells, my journey took me to San Carlos, on the San Carlos Apache Reservation.

J.K. Gresset, the District Superintendent, asked me to assist the older missionary couple there, Brother and Sister Silas Rexroat— two very kind, special people. In March 1968, Sister Cree took me and my few possessions to San Carlos. I had spent three months with the Crees; I will never forget their kindness to me.

So my adventure continued—quietly, as I was still regaining my strength, I started children's church, worked with the youth, and preached occasionally. The Rexroats were very considerate, and would often tell me, "You go rest—and don't get up early," —

though they were both very early risers.

Dear Brother Rexroat was one of those people who could hardly bring himself to throw anything away. I learned this one day after he asked me if I felt up to helping him clean out a small storage room. I told him I would, and I was astonished to find the room contained several dozen old electric motors of all sizes.

We took them outside, he carried the larger ones—carefully explaining that each one needed only this or that small part and it would work just fine. I had just finished sweeping the room, when Sister Rexroat called us to come in for lunch. As we finished eating, he said to me, "Now since you swept the room, we will carry all those motors back in and stack them neatly." I almost choked—I thought we would take them to the dump! Sister Rexroat laughed as she said, "Now you know why I wouldn't help him!" They left San Carlos not long after that—I often wondered what happened to all those old motors.

The Carrizo Years

Mamie and Jo Ann in their camp dresses.

I went home to Pennsylvania that summer for a visit. While I was there, Brother Gresset wrote and asked me to consider going to Carrizo, as he needed someone to minister to the people there. Thus, when I returned to Arizona, my journey took me back to the Fort Apache Reservation—to the very small remote village of Carrizo—to be the missionary in charge. I was joined by Mamie Beaver, who was a faithful co-worker for the rest of my years in Carrizo. Later she assisted me at the Indian Church in Winslow, Arizona. But that's another part of my journey.

Apache Singers

Leaders in Carrizo Church

Those years in Carrizo were happy ones with lots of adventures. I especially remember the trips to the Salt Banks. On one of those trips I was inspired to write an article "I Hear A Cry" for the *Pentecostal Evangel*, which is reprinted in this book. The article describes this hauntingly beautiful place and tells the Apache legend of the Salt Banks.

This would be a huge book if I told about all the things that happened, but some of my friends thought I should include the following "adventures."

Dear Old Bessie, A Special Woman

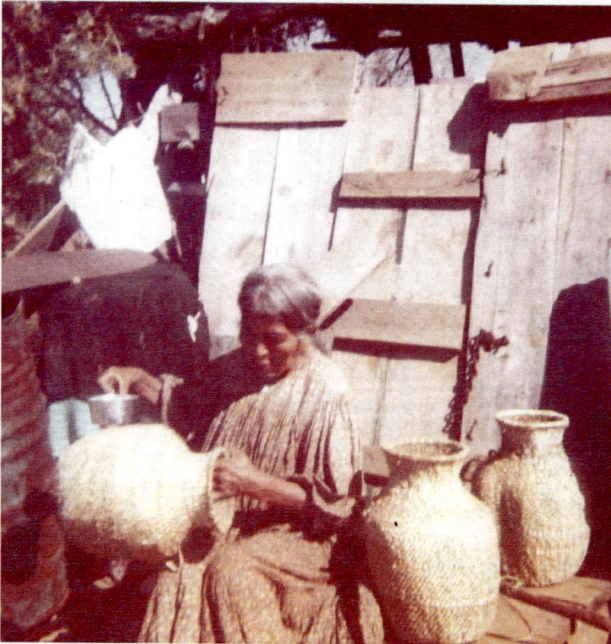

Bessie weaving Apache water jug.

In this book there are three stories about a wonderful older Apache woman—Bessie Truax. Bessie, who is now with the Lord, was the epitome of the old time Apache woman—except, Bessie knew Jesus.

I can still see her shuffling along with her walking stick, slowly coming across the footbridge to get to the church. We had a wooden footbridge because it was one of those times when the other means of crossing the creek, which consisted of two pipes covered with dirt, had been washed away in a flood. (I have included a story in this book, "A Real Bridge Over Corduroy Creek" about the creek and the bridges, or lack thereof.) Some of the men in the village built the footbridge, it was narrow and high, with no railings. Good thing I was on the side where the church was. I was scared to cross that bridge. But Bessie did. Bessie did not understand much English. Since nearly everyone else did, we did not interpret every service—regardless, Bessie always came to church.

I hope you enjoy the stories about her, they are: "The Old Weaver Remembers"; "Bessie's New House"; and "What Is His Name?"

How We Got A New Road

The main part of Carrizo is in the bottom of a canyon. When I first went there, the unpaved road ran straight down to the village and sometimes it was so muddy—so slick, we couldn't get out of the canyon. One time when I managed to get up the muddy road, on the return trip, I nearly slid over the edge. I had to leave my van there for several days, with rocks against the wheels to hold it.

The people had long wanted a new paved road. After I almost slid over the side of the canyon, a delegation led by Hoke, the medicine man, went to the tribal authorities to ask for a better road. Everyone laughed as they told me that the medicine man told the tribal leaders, "We have to have a better road—this one is too dangerous for the 'indaa saan'"—the old, white woman. That's what most of the people called me. As I was only in my thirties, I didn't take it as a compliment—until I found out it was a title of respect. They listened to the medicine man—we got a new road.

Me And The Medicine Man

The medicine man developed an infection in his feet and the government hospital in Whiteriver wanted to send him to the larger Indian hospital in Phoenix. He was afraid to go to Phoenix for fear they would amputate his feet. He refused to go until he could come back to Carrizo first. Because he said someone had told him in a dream that if the 'inashood, the Christians, in Carrizo would pray for him, he would be healed.

They brought him back and many of us gathered in his little house. We all "talked" to him. "Talking" is the Apache term for sternly telling someone what they need to do. Then we prayed for him. The next day they took him to Phoenix. In a few days he was back, walking around, good as new! Of course, we were happy about that. Then some of the people told us that he was saying it wasn't Jesus through the 'inashood's prayers who healed him. No, he had healed himself, by singing and blowing yellow powder on his feet. That's one of the ways a medicine man conducts a ceremony. I told the people, "We know who healed him. We'll just put it in the Lord's hands."

About two years later, on a cold winter evening just before time for the Wednesday night service, a pickup truck pulled into the church yard. The driver jumped out, ran to me and said, "The medicine man's little girl is real sick. He wants you to bring the people and pray for her. Get in, I'll take you to his house."

A bunch of us climbed into the back of the truck; but a few people had their own trucks and they came too, bringing more people with them. You may be sure, I was doing a lot of praying on that short drive to Hoke's house. When we got there, we found his little daughter lying on a mattress on the floor. Her face was red and sweaty, her eyes rolled back in her head that she kept turning from side to side. As she moaned softly, I put my hand on her forehead—it was very hot. She gave no indication that she knew we were there. Yes, I remember thinking, the medicine man's little girl is "real sick," indeed.

Hoke was begging us to pray. Suddenly, I knew what to say. Looking directly at him, I said, "No." There was a stunned silence in the room. I continued, "Hoke, when we prayed for you and Jesus healed your feet, I heard that you said you did it yourself. Is that true?"

Looking at the floor, he answered softly, "Yes."

"Now," I went on, "we will only pray for Janice, if you will promise us that when Jesus heals her, you will not say you did it with singing and yellow powder."

He raised his head, looked directly at me and quietly said, "I promise."

We prayed, I mean, we really prayed! When I finally opened my eyes, I was amazed. Janice was sitting up on the mattress, looking perfectly normal! She was pulling on her socks and shoes, laughing and saying, "I want to go to church." They all came to church that night. Hoke never came again but his wife and children continued to come.

Some time later Sister Alice, one of the faithful women of the church, came in to talk to us about something. In the course of the conversation, she asked with a very serious expression, "Do you know what Hoke is saying?"

Momentarily, I had a dreadful feeling. It was only momentarily; because I saw her eyes begin to twinkle. "No, I don't know," I answered.

She started laughing as she told us, that she had heard people saying that when they asked Hoke to sing and blow yellow powder, he would tell them, "I'll do it, but if you get healed, only Jesus can heal you!"

The year after I left Carrizo, Mamie was still there helping the young Apache man who was then pastor. Hoke got very sick. Mamie and some of the people went to see him in the hospital. He prayed with them to receive the Lord and he died shortly afterwards. I look forward to seeing Hoke in Heaven.

The Body Snatchers

There is a story in this book, "Wake in Apache Land," that describes the Apache custom of having a wake when someone dies. One of the funniest things I ever did was helping "snatch" a casket from a wake!

Here's how it happened. Brother Marcus, one of the faithful older men, knocked on the door one day with what seemed a reasonable request. The medicine man's wife had sent him to tell me her father had died. His body (in the casket) had been taken to her sister's place in Cedar Creek, a village about 12 miles away. But the wake was supposed to be at the medicine man's house, in Carrizo. Since they had no way to do it, would I please go get him—the body in the casket. Brother Marcus said he and his two sons, both middle-aged men, would go with me.

His sons were waiting outside. They were so sure I would do it; they had already taken the two back seats out of the van. We used the van to help the people in many ways. It wouldn't be the first time I had hauled a casket—but I usually hauled it to the cemetery.

Off we went. When we got to Cedar Creek they directed me where to go. As we pulled into the yard, I realized these people had everything set up for a wake.

Before I could say anything, Brother Marcus told me in a stern voice, "Turn around and back up there." He pointed to the porch where the casket set on the rough box, draped with a beautiful Pendleton blanket. The crepe paper streamers were up and artificial flowers were pinned to the sheet hanging behind the casket.

I didn't argue. I turned around and backed up. The two sons leaped out, leaving the back van doors open and ran to the porch. As Brother Marcus jumped out of the front seat where he always rode, he said, "You stay here, don't turn her off." He meant the van. You can bet I stayed there and I sure didn't "turn her off."

It must have been the element of surprise. There were maybe a dozen men and women standing around—all seemed frozen. I guess, like me, they couldn't believe what was happening. Brother Marcus' sons closed the casket and set it on the porch. Brother Marcus yanked the blanket and cover off the rough box, and the three of them put the casket and blanket in the rough box and quickly fastened the cover back on it. Then they picked it up and carried it, almost at a run, and slid it into the back of the van.

About then the yelling and screaming started. A very drunk woman, whom I recognized as the sister of the medicine man's wife, ran toward the van, crying loudly. Before they could close the doors, she jumped in on top of the casket on her stomach. One of Brother Marcus' sons crouched down alongside the casket. They slammed the van doors, and Brother Marcus and the other son jumped in the front with me. Brother Marcus looked at me and calmly said, "Lets go back to Carrizo."

So, we headed back to Carrizo, with the woman lying on the casket, wailing in my ear! I finally yelled, I had to yell as she was so loud, "I know you are sad, but please can you cry a little quieter?" She sniffed a few times, gulped a little, and quietly said, "Okay." I never heard another sound out of her all the way back to Carrizo.

I later discovered there was a dispute between the sisters as to where the wake would be held. However, there were no repercussions against us for "snatching" the body. In fact, both sisters and the medicine man asked me to come preach at the wake every night and to have the funeral service in the church.

Remembering those years, I have to say the people loved that old van. They called it Nellie. They said she could work hard, like a good Apache woman. Over the years we had many more amusing adventures with Nellie.

I Didn't Say I Was A Nun

Another humorous adventure. A couple, looking very troubled, came to the house. Both were carrying big boxes. I opened the door, they brought the boxes in, set them down and without a word went back to their truck and carried in two more. Then they told me, a "white" man stopped at their house one evening a few weeks ago and asked them to buy some books. He told them the books would be good for their children. They had two small children.

They gave him all the money they had, $5 and signed his paper. They said he asked for their address and where the father, Van, worked. He left some small colorful books. That's what they thought they had bought. "Our kids do like to look at the books," they said. Then last week they got these four big boxes of books. They showed me that they had only opened one box and handed me a book out of it. It was an encyclopedia! From a publisher I had never heard of.

They showed me a letter telling them how much money they had to pay every month for the next couple of years. Almost in tears, they said, "We can't do this. We don't even have any place to put all these books." That was certainly true. They lived in a house consisting of two tiny rooms. I said, "Well maybe you can send them back."

I looked at the letter that came with their payment book and saw a Phoenix address and phone number. When I called the number, they told me, "It's too late to return the books." I couldn't get them to relent. In fact, they said, "We know where Mr. Manuel (Van's last name) works. We will garnish his wages if he doesn't pay for the books."

True, Van had a job. He was one of the cowboys that looked after the Carrizo cattle for the tribal cattle association. Many Apache people have a few head of cattle; each owner has his own brand. Each district of the reservation has its own herd of cattle. The cowboys keep watch and care for the cattle. They do a round up in the spring and brand the new calves. Now that's something to see! In the fall they do another round up and take the cattle the owners want to sell to the reservation–wide cattle sale held every fall. Being a cowboy was hard and unglamorous work—not highly paid. Van didn't have a truck; sometimes he used one belonging to the association—as he did that day.

What to do? I knew that salesman had taken advantage of these people, but I felt helpless. I remember sitting there looking at that letter—with its fancy letterhead. Suddenly I noticed that their main office was in New Jersey, and the man listed as president had an Italian-sounding name.

Without saying a word to Mamie or Van and his wife, I grabbed the phone and called that number in New Jersey. Naturally, a secretary answered. I asked to speak to Mr. Whoever he was. When she asked who was calling, I said, "Tell him Sister Jo Ann, at a Mission in Arizona, would like to speak to him, please."

When he came on the line, I knew our prayers were answered. He practically gushed, "Hello, Sister, how are you? What can I do for you today, Sister?"

Mamie and Van and his wife watched with wide eyes. I could hardly keep a straight face. Speaking in a soft voice, trying to sound pious, I told him what one of his salesmen had done. I also told him I had called the Phoenix office and gotten only threats, otherwise I wouldn't have bothered him—that was all true.

He apologized profusely! He said, "Yes, return the boxes." He wanted my name and address; I told him I was Sister Jo Ann, at Carrizo Mission, Show Low, Arizona. I explained they brought the Carrizo mail down to the trading post from Show Low three times a week. He said he would send me money to pay the postage on the box that had been opened.

I thanked him—profusely! I was tempted to tell him I would light a candle for him. But when I hung up the phone, Mamie said, in a shocked voice, "He thought you were a nun!"

I answered, "Hey, I told him the exact truth. I am Sister Jo Ann, and this is Carrizo Mission." She just shook her head. I told Van and his wife to never, never sign any papers or give any money if another "white" man knocks on their door. And yes, Mr. Whoever he was sent the money to return the opened box.

He Did Ask For Matches

Here is another incident that I'll never forget. It could have been serious but just turned out to be funny. The way we unwittingly handled it probably stopped similar things from happening, once the story got around.

Virginia and children

One evening after church, a family needed a ride to another part of the reservation where they were staying. The wife, Virginia, and their children were waiting in our living room, while the dad, Tracy, put their blankets and other stuff in the van.

I was sitting at one end of our long, narrow living room; the front door was at the other end. Mamie was in the kitchen that opened into the living room. There was a soft knock on the front door. Thinking it was Tracy, I called out, "Come in."

The door opened and a young man that everyone called Magician, for reasons unknown to me, came staggering into the living room—obviously drunk and yelling something, partly in English and partly in Apache.

I jumped up and met him in the middle of the room. The only word I could understand was "matches." So I shouted, "Mamie, bring him some matches, quick." She did!

When she ran in with a handful of the farmer's matches we always used, he instantly seemed to get sober. He turned pale and backed up against the front door. By that time, Virginia and the kids were almost rolling on the floor with laughter. Mamie kept trying to give him the matches, but he refused them.

Then gasping with shock, he said very clearly, "I said, 'If I had some matches, I would set myself on fire and burn myself up!'" Then he opened the door and ran!

A New Door Opens

When I start to write about those long ago days, my mind is flooded with the faces of people. Many of them gone now; I can almost hear their soft voices, almost catch the echo of their laughter.

I thought I would never leave Apache Land—but that still small voice that led me there began to speak to me about the next place. I didn't know where that would be, but I knew He would open the door—and my journey would continue. I knew there would be more adventures ahead.

So, that very ordinary day in Carrizo, when the phone rang as it had hundreds of times before, I answered—and at the end of the conversation, I gently hung up the phone, fighting back tears. I knew that phone call signaled the end of life as I had known it for nearly 10 years. A new door was opening.

The phone call was from the District Superintendent of Southern Idaho. He told me they desperately needed a missionary pastor in Fort Hall. He had called the Division of Home Missions in Springfield, Missouri, for help and they had recommended me. I was astonished—yet I knew, even as he spoke, that this would be the next stop on my journey.

Parting—A Sweet Sorrow

Lloyd and Viola

Lloyd and Viola, one couple among many whose lives I had seen totally transformed by the gospel, gave one of their cows to be barbecued for a wonderful farewell dinner. Several hundred people came from across the reservation and even from San Carlos, roughly 80 miles away. I cannot remember all of the lovely gifts I received—but the kind words and the tears are still in my heart.

Mamie opted to stay in Carrizo. We had both felt for sometime that the Lord was preparing a fine mature Apache man, Arnold Lupe, to follow me. He was married and had two children, and that spring he would graduate from American Indian College. Arnold had preached and filled in for us for the past three years. Both he and the people knew he would be their pastor someday. When it came about, he asked Mamie to stay to continue the ministry to the children and oversee the Sunday School.

Fort Hall

My adventures in Fort Hall were quite different—I went from a remote reservation setting to a small town, only 10 miles from the large city of Pocatello. A dear older friend, Susie Witt, accompanied me to Fort Hall and stayed about two months. Then Gary and Jo Ann Coleman came to assist me.

New Kids in Sunday School

Fort Hall is home to both the Shoshone and Bannock people. They had been teepee dwellers even though everyone now had a house. However, teepees were still used in ceremonies and on many other occasions. Sometimes when someone died, they put up a teepee and put the casket in it along with some chairs. Visitors would respectfully sit out there for awhile, usually in silence—quite different from an Apache wake.

The congregation in Fort Hall was small—14 people, my first Sunday. That included, Susie and me, and Pearl Barngrover, who came from American Falls to play the piano for us on Sundays. However, Julie was there—I remember she met me outside the church that first Sunday morning, her countenance glowing, as she said, "Welcome to Fort Hall, Sister Craver, we have been pray-ing for you."

Julie helped me with visitation and with her at my side, the doors opened. Thank God, with Julie's help, our numbers started to increase. You may read her remarkable testimony in this book; it was the basis for an article, "Shall We Leave Them Alone?" The Division of Home Missions reprinted that article in pamphlet form several times, to promote Native American Missions.

Julie and her husband, Richard

We printed a monthly bulletin and distributed it across the reservation. It had news, prayer requests, a short devotional, and announcements of upcoming church activities—such as the free prayer breakfast held one Saturday morning each month.

Gary and the Royal Rangers

We went on outings, had special fun times, and started Royal Rangers and Missionettes. The Lord blessed our efforts and soon we had so many who were eager to come to church that we couldn't get them all in the van. The district helped us buy a small, used school bus. My assistant Gary, was the driver. Better yet, we had new families coming on their own, bringing their children. We planned a Christmas program. The unexpected turn that program took is in an article I wrote called, "Never Alone At Christmas." You may read it in this book. Another article that I wrote while I was in Fort Hall, "Do You Listen Well?" is also in this book.

I don't think I ever worked as hard, before or since. By the time I left, a year or so later, we were averaging about 60. Yes, even though I knew the Lord sent me to Fort Hall, I also knew it would only be for a season.

My Journey Continues

Alvin Oya, who headed the American Indian Fellowship in Western Washington, came to Fort Hall to share with me his vision for a training center for Native People in the Northwest. He invited me to be part of it, assuring me there would be ministry for me until the training center came about. After prayer, I had peace that this was the next part of my journey. When I left Fort Hall, Gary and Jo Ann Coleman stepped into the pastoral role.

I moved to Pacific Beach near Taholah, a Native American town on the Quinault Reservation. The lady pastor and people of the Bible Light House Church in Taholah gave me a warm welcome. I often preached there when I was not holding teacher-training seminars or preaching in the other Indian churches. Though I was busy, I still had time to rest and regain my strength. After about a year, I did not see any progress toward the training center. So, when the District Superintendent of Arizona asked me to return to Arizona to be the missionary pastor of the Indian Church in Winslow—I heard that "still. small voice" in my heart, telling me, "Go!" The Superintendent suggested I ask Mamie to join me. I did—and she agreed. So my adventures continued.

Winslow, With The Navajos And Hopis

Little Navajo girl in traditional dress,
holding Navajo Bible

Winslow, a small city along I-40, has a sizable Indian population—mainly Navajo and Hopi people from the closest reservations. However, people from other tribes live there too. They all come in search of employment, which is scarce on Indian reservations. Living in this city was very different than living out on the reservation would have been. It was even different than living in Fort Hall—a predominately Indian town.

There was a small, yet strong, nucleus of faithful believers in the Winslow church, mainly Navajos, along with two older Hopi couples. However, the church needed teachers and leaders. It was a challenge to encourage and train the people, especially the new people the Lord brought in—but He helped us to do so.

The Navajos

The Navajo Reservation is the largest in the country—bigger than the state of West Virginia. All our Navajo people "lived" in Winslow, but the reservation was home to them—and so a mass exodus usually occurred every Friday. I used to say, "I am going to build a fence around Winslow, and lock the gate every Friday evening!"

However, the Lord added to the church many wonderful, faithful Navajo people. I think of Starr, a lovely young woman, who started bringing her children to Sunday School, because as a child she had attended the church. In time, Starr became the teacher of the teen class.

There was Dale and his family. We had a call to go pray for a man in the hospital—it was Dale, he was away from God, but that day he gave his life back to the Lord. When he got out of the hospital, he and his family came faithfully to church. I found out he could read Navajo.

The Wycliffe translators had put Navajo into writing many years earlier. All of the Navajos carried a Navajo Bible, but none could read it. Dale started a Navajo reading class—we advertised it in the local paper—it was an instant success! Dale also became our adult Sunday School teacher. He taught in English as by then we had people from various tribes, as well as an elderly Hispanic man, some Anglo people, and an African American family. Speaking of which—the Lord also sent us an African American man, a school teacher, to be our pianist. We also started a Navajo-speaking Sunday School class for the several non-English speakers who started coming.

Learning Navajo

Brother Dale, teaching Sunday School

Navajo people are renowned for their art work, silver and turquoise jewelry, and for the rugs they weave. We had artists, silversmiths and weavers in the church and were blessed with gifts from them. I especially cherish a rug that was made for me by a dear elderly lady we called Grandma Tsosie.

Navajo Crafts & Grandma Tsosie

Grandma Tsosie and her daughter came into town to live one winter. They were in town because the daughter, who was far from young, was on dialysis. In the winter the unpaved roads on the reservation got so muddy, sometimes they couldn't get to town for her treatments.

Someone told us about them, said they were Christians, and that they would like to come to church. I went to visit them and started picking them up for the services.

Grandma made my rug herself, from scratch, as the saying goes. She did not speak any English. Pointing to the pile of wool on the floor beside her, she told her daughter, "Tell my little sheep (her special name for me—though I was far from little) this wool is from my own sheep." Many Navajo people who live on the reservation have sheep. Mutton is their favorite meat—as beef is for Apaches—but like all the tribes I have known, they each make their traditional fry bread.

Back to Grandma—in the days that followed, she prepared the wool, cleaning it, carding it, and then spinning it into yarn on a small stick-type instrument that she twirled by hand. She dyed the yarn, with dye made from plants she had gathered—no stuff bought at the trading post for Grandma's rug! She wove the rug on a handmade loom. I wondered what the pattern would be, so I asked her daughter to ask Grandma about it. She answered in Navajo, with a laugh, as she tapped the side of her head. Her daughter told me, she said to tell you the design is in her head, it will come out on the loom.

My rug, which is gold, black, gray and the natural white of the wool, is in a diamond design. I never wrote about Grandma and the rug, but I have used it for many an illustrated sermon. One example: God knows the pattern for our lives, He weaves it on the loom of life, and the dark things that happen help make the design beautiful—so trust Him. Before another winter, we heard that both the daughter and Grandma had died. It will be wonderful to talk with them in Heaven. Grandma and I will understand each other there!

Grandma Tsosie in front of her loom with my rug!

The Dark Side

Though we lived in this small city, we encountered the dark side of Navajo culture—curses and witchcraft, including skin walkers! The latter are people who cover themselves with a coyote skin and, under demonic power, do terrible things.

I recall three little girls—maybe 8 through 12, who started coming to church. They had wonderful salvation experiences and were filled with the Holy Spirit.

One night after service they said they had to talk to me. They told me a "hair-raising" story about a skin walker who had started coming around their house late at night, even climbing on the roof—howling. They said the next morning after this "thing" had been there, they found lots of coyote tracks—they were terrified.

The girls did not want me to come to their house, or to tell anyone, as their unsaved parents would not have liked that. I prayed with them. Then I told them, "Tomorrow evening before it gets dark, take your Bible, go outside and walk around your house." I told them to say, "In the name of Jesus, by the power of His Word and His blood, we command every evil spirit to go away from here and never come back."

I doubt if they remembered my exact words—but the next time they came to church, they excitedly told me, "We did it, Sister Craver, and it has not come back!"

Later, when their parents got saved, they said they knew the Lord delivered them from the skin walker through the girl's prayer. And it never did come back! Before I left Winslow, the oldest of those girls, Marthalen, was crowned a Missionette Honor Star!

Marthalen, The Honor Star

Is It Real?

You may ask, "Are these things real?" And I ask you, "Is the devil real?" Believe me, the powers of darkness are real indeed. They are especially real among a people who have never known the life-changing power of the Holy Spirit. In regard to curses, an older couple, Leo and Sadie, came to the house one day, begging to use the phone. I allowed them to do so. It was raining that day and I could tell he was in pain—he could hardly walk, so I took them back to their home.

They told me a sad story. He was retired from the railroad, and also had a veteran's pension and a new pickup truck. They said the reason he was in such pain was because some of his relatives went to a medicine man and had a curse put on him. These relatives had taken his truck and every month when he got his checks, they came to town and demanded most of the money—leaving them barely enough to survive on.

These relatives told him if he didn't do what they said, he would get worse. He had been to many doctors and they knew he was losing the use of his legs and was in lots of pain, but they couldn't figure out why and, of course, he didn't tell them.

Neither of them had ever been saved, though she said she went to a church when she was a child in boarding school. In years past, most reservation children were taken to government-run boarding schools when they were very young. The government still operates some boarding schools on the Navajo Reservation. I have heard many horror stories about life in boarding schools, especially from older Indian people—when conditions were much worse than today.

Leo and Sadie started coming to church and after a few weeks, they both gave their hearts to the Lord. I well remember that Sunday morning—Leo was instantly set free from pain! I told him, and even though he understood English very well, I had Dale repeat to him in Navajo, "Your relatives no longer have any power over you. As long as you love Jesus and serve Him, their curses cannot hurt you. Tell your relatives about Jesus, and tell them to leave your truck here, or you will call the police and don't give them any money."

Well, he did just that! From then on, they came faithfully to church in their nice truck. When they found out about tithing, they gladly paid their tithes. Leo always called me "Grandmother!" I knew it was a title of respect. Every Sunday Leo's testimony was, "I am all right now, Grandmother, Jesus makes me all right!"

The Hopi

*One of the Hopi Christians
in the Winslow church*

The Hopi are a smaller tribe whose reservation in the high desert country of northern Arizona is completely surrounded by the vast Navajo Reservation. They live either in pueblo-type villages atop three rugged mesas or in modern housing around the mesas. Known as the peaceful ones, the Hopi have the distinction of being the oldest dwellers in this land—reaching back a millennium.

They are farmers, raising corn, which plays a major role in their traditional beliefs, along with beans, squash and melons. The Hopi are also silversmiths, basket and rug weavers, artists and wood carvers—but they are mainly known for their beautiful pottery. They are a friendly, hospitable people. In Winslow, when we went out knocking on doors to reach new people, we knew immediately if the people on whose door we knocked were Hopi, because they would call out, "Come in!" Once inside, they offered us either something to eat or drink. In contrast, people from other tribes would sometimes peek out the window, then if they opened the door—they came outside, closed the door behind them and talked to us.

Yet, the Hopi are the most traditional of Indians, having retained more of the religious and social practices of their ancestors than any other Arizona tribe. Their lives revolve around a religious calendar of ceremonies. The Kachina dolls they carve can be found in stores across the southwest. The dolls represent the "Kachina," their gods, and there are over 300 different Kachinas!

Protestant missionaries have struggled to reach the Hopi for at least a century—Catholics were there in the early 1600's. In the late 1950's, Rowena Chaves and Jewel Barnett pioneered the Assembly of God church in Polacca, meaning *butterfly*, a village at the base of First Mesa. The church has never been large—it's not easy to be a Christian in the land of the Hopi.

Angels—Winslow Christmas program

Being aware of this, we were pleased to find Hopi people in the Winslow church. In the course of time, the Lord brought in a few more and some Hopi children started coming to Sunday School. In this book you may read, Hold Onto The Book, based on an amazing story a Hopi woman told us one night in a Bible study.

Same Journey, Different Path

I spent nearly four, happy years in Winslow. The next phase of my journey started with physical problems, followed by surgery, followed by a year off from active missionary service. I spent most of that year in the home of Ruth Walker, a dear friend in Southern California.

I was then asked by the Division of Home Missions to take over the ministry of Pauline Masteries, who was retiring. Pauline coordinated the International Correspondence Institute (ICI) outreach to Native Americans.

This invitation did not come as a total surprise. Pauline had once stayed a few nights with us in Winslow when visiting Indian churches in the area. While she was there, the Holy Spirit revealed to me that someday the ICI outreach would be my ministry. I never told anyone—but, in the course of time, it came to pass!

The ICI Years

The main thrust of the ICI program consisted of two sets of six free lessons, mailed individually, followed by two series of books sent for a small fee. A certificate was issued upon completion of each set of lessons and each book.

The lessons had a space in the back for referrals—in this way the outreach multiplied. I also visited Indian churches far and wide, enrolling people in the lessons. In some churches I taught some of the books, adjusting their content to fit the culture of the Native people..

The lessons, especially the first set, "The Great Questions of Life," were powerful. They reached Indian people—in a phenomenal way, because people could read and think about what the lesson said in the privacy of their homes. I received many testimonies telling me how the lessons answered questions they had been afraid to ask or didn't know who to ask.

The lesson, "What Happens After Death," especially drew lots of comments—touching the hearts and minds of hundreds of Indian people. I once received a note from a Navajo woman asking if she could keep the last lesson her daughter completed; it was the one that dealt with what happens after death. She said, her daughter had written on the lesson that she understood it and had prayed to accept the Lord—that afternoon she was killed in a car accident.

My adventures in these years usually had to do with what came in my mail. I often felt like a spiritual "Dear Abby." Many people wrote letters in the lessons they returned—asking for advice about personal problems or questions about scriptures.

I was involved in this ministry for about 10 years. In that time I sent out over a hundred thousand lessons along with hundreds of books across this nation, as well as into Canada. Over ten thousand people received certificates. After all these years, sometimes an Indian person will come up to me and say, "Remember me? I did the lessons you sent and I am still serving the Lord!" I expect to meet many Indian people in Heaven whose lives were impacted by those lessons.

An Exciting Development

In 1984, shortly after I started my ministry with ICI, the Convocation of Christian Indian Leaders was founded by Indian ministers. The "Convocation"—an annual meeting held in a different part of the country each year—usually lasts several days, with special speakers and workshops. It is open to anyone involved in ministry to Native Americans. I did everything I could to support and encourage this meeting and the Indian leaders involved in it.

In 1988, at the Convocation in Mobridge, South Dakota, it was a challenge and a privilege, to be asked by these Indian leaders to help establish the Native American Christian Resource Center to publish a magazine for Native Americans. Four of us were involved in this exciting adventure. I was the editor; Phyllis Bowersock, a missionary; and Carlita Billy, a Native American minister, were my assistants. Duane Hammond, another missionary, was in charge of layout and publishing. Like myself, Duane had long desired to see such a publication and had, in fact, tried to start one a few years previously.

Native Pentecostal News (NPN) Is Born!

Phyllis Bowersock

Carlita Billy

In the months following the meeting in Mobridge, we published the first issue calling it simply *"Convocation News."* Then in 1989, during the Convocation in Phoenix, Arizona the Indian people chose the name for their new magazine: *"Native Pentecostal News!"* Talk about a walk of faith—taking on the responsibility of publishing this quarterly magazine was that! For several years we did not have a central office. Phyllis and I used to say, "Have computer, will travel." Because, at the time Phyllis and her husband were working among the Navajos in Northern Arizona—Duane was a missionary pastor in New Mexico. Carlita lived in a different part of New Mexico, and I lived in East Central Arizona, several hundred miles from everyone else. We all continued in our ministries, driving many miles every month or so, to meet in various places to work on the upcoming issue. Looking back, I wonder how we did it.

NPN, as we always referred to it, quickly became a successful tool for communication among the Native churches. Most missionaries soon got behind us—though it took awhile to convince some of our "old line" missionaries that NPN was not a threat. Its teaching articles and testimonies made NPN an outstanding tool for evangelism. With rare exceptions, like my occasional editorial article, all of our material was written by Native Americans and, of course, Native Americans did the artwork. The picture on the cover of this book was the cover of the Summer 1999 edition of NPN.

My Journey Leads Me To The Big City—Phoenix!

After publishing NPN "on the road" for a few years, the people in the Assemblies of God Home Missions Department thought the Native Resource Center needed a central office. They suggested we move to Phoenix, and they asked the American Indian College to give us office space, which they did. So, in 1992, I took courage in hand and in fear and trembling, I moved to the "Big City!" The rest of "the gang" moved the following year.

Let me tell you about my move to the "Big City." I had always lived either on a reservation or in small urban areas, so moving to Phoenix was a "real adventure!" I made the 200-plus mile trip to Phoenix where a friend helped me look for an apartment. We had been looking for about a week when one day she said, "Let's go up this street; there are nice apartments here on Rose Lane, they rarely have a vacancy, but let's look."

Mr. Spitz and me and front of my "Big City" home!

We drove up Rose Lane and, lo and behold, there was a for rent sign! The apartment door was open, we looked in and an elderly little Jewish man, said "Come in!" He was the owner and was there with some workmen who were painting. When I walked in and looked around, I felt a peace from the Lord. I knew, "this is it!" I told the owner, Mr. Spitz, that I wanted to rent it. He quoted me a very reasonable price and accepted my check. We signed the rental agreement—it was a "done deal." I was now a city girl!

That evening, Mrs. Spitz called me. She was not happy. She thought her husband should have done a background check on me before accepting my money and putting his signature on the rental agreement.

Mrs. Spitz conducted a verbal background check on me right then. She demanded, "You gonna have a live-in boyfriend?" I said, "No."

"You got any pets?" I said, "No, I don't even have a goldfish!"

"No dogs? No cats?" She persisted. "Nothing," I replied, "just me!"

"Well okay," she muttered. Later, when I was moving in she came by to visit and decided she liked me! I lived there for the next 14 years. When the Spitz's sold the place, the new owner kept raising the rent. Finally, the Lord made it possible, another miracle, for me to put the down payment on the condo where I live today!

My ministry with ICI came to an end about three years after I moved to Phoenix. The office in Springfield who printed the lessons, changed their format. Rather than six individual lessons, they put them all in a booklet of about 70 pages. I found it almost impossible to get Native people to read, work through and mail back a booklet that size. However, I continued teaching the ICI books in Indian churches until I retired in 1999.

Louisa Lee Navajo Artist for NPN

Back to NPN—we started printing tracts—testimonies of Native Americans. Light for the Lost funded the printing cost of the tracts and a booklet for new converts, titled: "*A New Trail*." In addition to the regular magazine, we printed a "Special Edition" once a year—also funded by Light For The Lost and used for evangelism. We charged a small subscription fee for NPN, but we mailed out the tracts for the cost of the postage. In a few years, Indian churches across the nation were subscribing—a number of them were non-Pentecostal!

Jimmy Yellowhair

About three years after moving to Phoenix, Duane felt he should return to pastoral ministry in New Mexico. When he left, the Lord sent us Jimmy Yellowhair, a Navajo man with great computer skills. Jimmy and his wife lived in Flagstaff, she was pastor of the Indian Assembly and he worked for Northern Arizona University. He made the long trip to Phoenix each quarter to help us with the layout. Jimmy had a desire to write teaching material for Native people. Light for the Lost funded a booklet containing 12 lessons that Jimmy wrote and illustrated and which we printed and distributed.

Circumstances changed at the Bible College; they needed the space we were using. We took another step of faith and rented a small apartment to use as an office for the Native American Christian Resource Center. These were sometimes difficult, but always rewarding, days of ministry.

My Journey Changes Direction—Again

George and Rita Kallappa

In 1997, we felt it was time to put NPN in the hands of a capable Native couple—George Kallappa, and his wife, Rita. George is a member of the Makah tribe, from Neah Bay, Washington. He is a well known Native minister, having evangelized in Indian churches for many years. For three years George and Rita did a great job! NPN grew exponentially—with many new subscribers in almost every state as well as Canada—and more tracts were printed.

By the time George handed over the Resource Center in the fall of 2000, (to some people who were not happy with his leadership), over a half million tracts had been printed and distributed. The people who forced them out, tried to continue NPN, but, unfortunately, it and the tract ministry soon faded away. The death of NPN was a great loss for the Native people and a deep personal grief for me. But God! He knows how to bind up the broken hearted. He had a whole new and exciting path planned for me!

Retired, Refired—The Journey... And The Adventures, Continue!

In 2000, I received my honorary retirement status. Someone asked me, "What does that mean?" My answer: "I don't have to send in any more reports!"

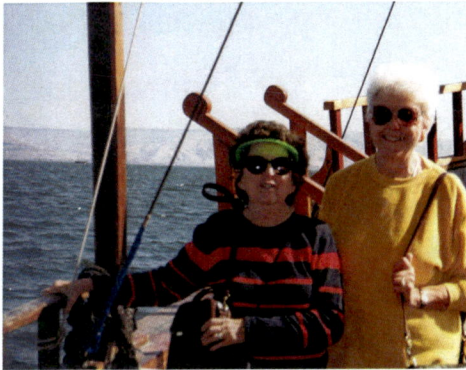

Ruth Walker and me on the
Sea of Galilee—in a boat, not walking

Almost immediately after I "retired," the Lord began to make it possible for me to make trips to Israel and several other countries: Jordan, Turkey, Greece and the Greek Isles, including Patmos, as well as Poland and Switzerland, and two weeks in London and Wales. I am amazed at the goodness of God!

I have been to Israel seven times! Not seven "tours," although, there were a few of those; but I have been blessed to be able to stay in Jerusalem for a month to six weeks at a time on four different occasions.

Outdoor café in Jerusalem

While in "The Land," as many Jewish people refer to Israel, I have traveled by car from Eilat to Mount Hermon. In fact, I have been privileged to see much of that marvelous land. I not only rode the tram to the top of Masada, I also flew over it in a small plane!

From these trips the Lord has led me into the study of prophecy. He has helped me write several series of lessons that I teach in both Indian and non-Indian churches. In addition to the teaching series, I preach wherever I am invited.

I am now 75 years old and these lines from that wonderful old hymn say it all:

The Lord has promised good to me…
His word my hope secures.
He will my shield and portion be…
as long as life endures.

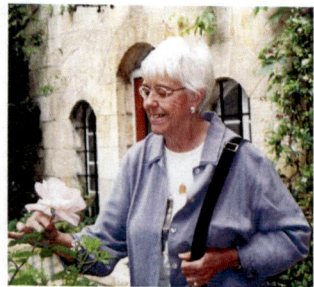

"The greatest adventure is what lies ahead…"

Convocation of
Christian Indian Leaders

Reverend Jo Ann Craver
is hereby recognized for her outstanding years of faithful
Christian service to Native American ministry.
Awarded at Hungry Horse Montana, June 16, 1998.

Home Missionary Receives Honor

Jo Ann Craver was awarded a beautiful plaque for her dedication and commitment to Home Missionary work among the Native Americans. The plaque reads:

On the occasion of the
MISSION AMERICA CONFERENCE 1998
JO ANN CRAVER
is hereby presented this
Citation of Excellence
for your 30 years of faithful service as a Nationally
Appointed Home Missionary.
July 30, 1998

The Native Christian Resource Center, along with the many churches in which she ministered congratulate her for her recognition by the Assemblies of God Organization. Her "Pride and Joy" is in the founding of the Native Christian Resource Center, which produces the Native Pentecostal News, and a number of tracts that deal with the conversion of Native Americans. We love you, Jo Ann!

Reprinted from Native Pentecostal News
George Kallappa, Editor

Now For The Rest Of The Book

In the rest of the book you may read articles I wrote, which were printed in various Assemblies of God publications, that span the years of my ministry to Native Americans. They will give you a glimpse of the places, the people, and some of the adventures that were part of my journey. Some of the articles are of a devotional nature—though I managed to work something about Native Americans into most of them. But then, Native Americans have been the focus of my life for many years.

Though written a number of years ago the article, *Wake in Apache Land*, is still a basically accurate description of wakes held on the Fort Apache Reservation—very little has changed.

The article, *Shall We Leave Them Alone*, Julie Coby's amazing testimony was reprinted at least three times by the Division of Home Missions and used to promote Native American Ministry. The need it outlines remains virtually unchanged—though we have more Native people involved in ministry—the percentage of Native Americans who consider themselves Christians is very low. The last I remember reading it was less than 10 percent. Something to consider: On the Tohono O'odham Reservation, the second largest one in the nation, located in the southeastern desert of Arizona, there are at least 60 small villages, with possibly only six small full gospel works.

The Day I prayed for a Vacuum Cleaner, was the first article I sent to the Pentecostal Evangel. I still remember my amazement, and joy, when it was accepted. It appeared on the back of the July 15, 1973 issue. The article, *A Miracle For Me*, was written about an experience I had while living in Carrizo, Arizona, working with the White Mountain Apaches. It was published after I moved to Fort Hall, Idaho. When I think about that story, I am still amazed about what happened to me that day. What an awesome God we serve!

Three of the four Christmas stories you will find in this book were written while I was in Carrizo. Christmas was always an exciting time there. The fourth story is about the unexpected Christmas program experience I had in Fort Hall. And yes, I still have the beautiful hair barrette!

The God Who Loves Us, is my only work of fiction, it was a two part story in the September 13th and 20th 1993 issues of Junior Trails. In it I incorporate things I was told by older Apache people, like the little girl running to the creek and jumping in every morning—they did this even in the winter. I recall one older lady telling me how the icicles that formed in her hair jingled like bells as she ran back to the wickiup.

May you find these to be "articles of lasting interest." And may the Lord give you a new understanding of Native Americans, their lives and their spiritual needs.

Native Ministry Continues...

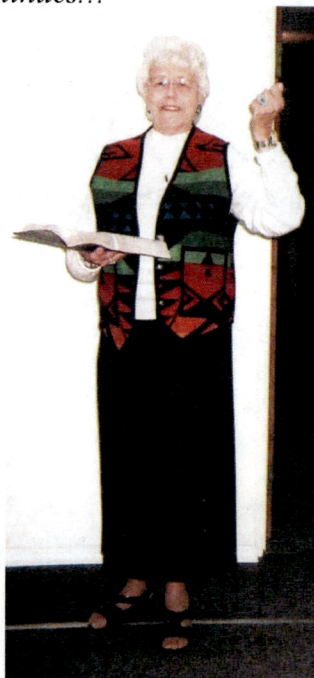

LIST OF ARTICLES

A MIRACLE, FOR ME?

'God help me! I can't see the road!'

Do you believe in miracles? Do you think God intervenes in our very natural and sometimes mundane lives with supernatural power?

I used to believe in miracles for other people; I classed them with freak accidents or the chicken pox. I never expected a miracle to happen to me.

Let me tell you the experience I had as a missionary to the American Indians while living in a small Apache village on the Fort Apache Reservation in Arizona.

It was our custom to have a Watch Night service on New Year's Eve. We would share testimonies, sing, and read promises from the Bible. Shortly before midnight we would kneel at the altar and partake of Holy Communion. Our Indian brothers and sisters in Christ found this a beautiful way to end one year and begin another.

A miracle happened one New Year's Eve when I had forgotten to buy grape juice for the Communion service. There is one small store in the village, but grape juice was not to be found on its sparsely stocked shelves.

The nearest off-reservation town where we could shop was Show Low about 25 miles northeast. An excellent highway goes into Show Low. It is usually a lovely drive through scenic mountain meadows and tall pines. The elevation climbs nearly 2,000 feet between Carrizo, the village where we lived, and Show Low. But this morning the clouds were dark and threatening; a strong wind was blowing. Furthermore, the weather service predicted heavy snow and high wind. A travelers warning was being broadcast.

I knew that warning should be heeded, but I struggled within myself. Should I go? If I went and had trouble in the coming storm, I knew there was no place up that long road to get help except one small store 8 miles out of Show Low. It probably would not be open that day.

But how could I disappoint the faithful Christian Indians when they gathered for the service that night?

The conviction that I should go to Show Low and get the grape juice grew stronger. When a few weak rays of sunlight penetrated the gray clouds around 10 a.m., my courage rose. "I am going to Show Low," I told my co-worker. Once the decision was made I felt relieved. Hurriedly I got ready and soon was on the way.

The first miles were uneventful. The road was clear, though the wind was strong. As I climbed higher into the mountains I ran into the predicted snow. Soon the road was covered. The few cars I met moved at a snail's pace.

The windshield on our van was cracked, and this did not help my visibility as I crept along in the thickly falling snow.

I dared not stop, and there was no place to turn around. Then I thought of the wide space along the road at the reservation boundary line; perhaps I could turn around there. But that was only a few miles out of Show Low. If I could make it that far, why not go on?

Please, Lord, show me what I should do, I prayed.

When I reached the reservation boundary line, the choice was made for me. A snow plow had been along earlier and left the road edged with high banks of snow on both sides. I had to go on!

Finally I reached Show Low and parked at the store. I quickly bought the grape juice and hurried out to the van. Now to get back to Carrizo, I thought.

I bowed my head and prayed briefly, but fervently, for a safe trip home. As I drove, my windshield wipers were going at high speed. I also had the heater, the defroster, and the fan all on high. But after a while I realized they were not doing the job. The cracks in the windshield were holding the moisture; ice was forming. Soon only a small area was clear enough to see through.

"Please, Lord, keep that place clear so I can tell where I am going," I prayed aloud.

A glance in the rearview mirror showed dim lights far behind me. They were the headlights of other cars, barely visible in the storm.

It was snowing harder now, and the wind was so strong I had trouble controlling the van. Swirling snow seemed to be coming straight at me.

Suddenly I was lost in white nothingness! Though the small space was still clear on the windshield, I could not tell where the road was in the blowing snow.

Automatically I started to touch my brake. Oh, no! I thought, I can't stop! The cars following me would never see me in time to stop safely.

I could feel panic rising within me. I fought against it by crying aloud, "Oh, God, help me, help me; I can't see the road."

For a long moment, time seemed to be suspended. The van was still moving slowly through the white void. I couldn't see a thing. Then directly in front of me, as I strained to see, I could make out what appeared to be black tire tracks!

Black tire tracks! Just as if a car were in front of me making tracks, through that deep snow, right down to the pavement! I steered the van into those tracks. They were all I could see in the blowing snow.

Slowly at first, then faster, I drove in those clear black tracks. I trembled as I realized I was driving on bare black pavement through that awful storm!

A glance in the rearview mirror showed no tracks behind me— only a blank whiteness. I tasted the salty tears before I realized I was crying. Aloud I thanked the Lord for showing me the road.

I kept praising the Lord and just followed those clear tracks until the storm abated. When I could again see the road clearly, the tracks faded away.

Our Watch Night service was well attended. When we gathered around the altar to partake of Holy Communion, our Lord's familiar words, "This do in remembrance of me," held very special meaning for me.

I would always remember how my wonderful Lord showed me the road in the midst of the storm. A miracle, for me!

A REAL BRIDGE OVER CORDUROY CREEK

Corduroy Creek flows through this canyon where I live. It is usually no more than a placid brook.

But heavy snow comes to the high country, this part of Arizona where the elevation climbs above the 7,000-foot mark. When the thaw begins or when we get a prolonged rain, Corduroy Creek becomes a raging river.

When I came here, there was no real bridge over Corduroy Creek—just two large pipes covered with rocks and dirt. One end was dangerously caved in, leaving just enough width for the wheels of the car. One must cross the creek to reach the highway. Each time I drove over that high narrow dirt bridge, I felt as Queen Esther did when she went before the king: "If I perish, I perish."

I prayed much about that makeshift bridge. I wrote to friends to pray with me for a real bridge.

The Lord heard! That summer the government agency brought in men and equipment, and in an unbelievably short time we had a real bridge!

Oh, it looked beautiful with its large concrete abutments at each end, and one large concrete support in the center. True, it had no railings and only a metal grating for flooring, but it was enough. And it was a real bridge!

A year went by, an unusually dry year for Arizona. When fall came the next year, we had an early snow, then a few warm days.

One morning I awoke to the sound of hard steady rain. I wasn't worried. We had a real bridge, so let it rain. It did—all day. By early afternoon people were gathering down by the bridge.

My co-worker and I bundled into our raincoats and boots and set out through a sea of mud to join the people at the bridge. Until you've waded through sticky adobe mud, you really don't know what mud is. It clings to your boots until your feet become so heavy you can hardly lift them.

We finally made it to the bridge where the people who live on our side of the creek—all Apache Indians (my co-worker and I are the only non-Indians in this canyon) were watching the rising water in forlorn silence. The water was even now lapping at the iron grating of the bridge floor. Small logs and debris riding on the rushing current were swept under the bridge and emerged on the other side.

At least the bridge will stand. I comforted myself with that thought.

The water would subside, and the bridge, that beautiful real bridge, would still be there.

However, the water did not subside; it continued to rise! We had to keep backing up as the water crept higher and higher.

"Look! look!" someone shouted. The water had cut under the road at both ends of the bridge. Before our startled eyes the road crumbled into the raging water.

At about the same time a large tree came riding on the crest of the water. It lodged against the bridge. More and more logs and debris became jammed against the tree and the bridge.

"It can't stand long," someone said. They were right. Soon we heard a groaning sound, then a mighty roar. The bridge, my beautiful real bridge, was gone!

We were isolated for several days. The water finally did go down. The government and tribal offices sent in workers to bulldoze what was left of the crumpled cement abutments. It was back to the pipes and dirt and rock fill for a makeshift bridge again.

During the next year and a half, we had a lot of high water which left us isolated several days or even a week or two at a time.

So it was a glad day for us when we heard they planned to build another real bridge. This time a contractor came from Phoenix with men and equipment. They brought in a pile driver and began to dig a foundation for the concrete abutments.

"The problem with the other bridge," the foreman explained, "was an improper foundation for the abutments. One must go down to the bedrock, or the bridge will not stand the floods. The first bridge, though it had looked strong and beautiful, was built on the sand. That's why it collapsed."

It was like hearing a paraphrase of the words of Jesus in Matthew 7:24-27: "Therefore whosoever heareth these sayings of mine, and doeth them, I will liken him unto a wise man, which built his house upon a rock; and the rain descended, and the floods came, and the winds blew, and beat upon that house; and it fell not: for it was founded upon a rock.

"And everyone that heareth these sayings of mine, and doeth them not, shall be likened unto a foolish man which built his house upon the sand: and the rain descended, and the floods came, and the winds blew, and beat upon that house; and it fell: and great was the fall of it."

Here Jesus talked about the importance of the proper foundation. That proper foundation, the Rock, is none other than Christ himself. "All other ground," as the songwriter put it, "is sinking, sand."

There are many sand foundations that look good. Human philosophy, education, ancient wisdom, good works, religion, culture, are a few. But none of these will stand the test of Matthew 7:25. Jesus said the rain would come—the steady pounding rain of worry, trouble, the incessant cares of life that drive people relentlessly. He said there would be floods —devastation, catastrophe, death, loss of property or job, a dozen other things that can suddenly enter any life.

The winds will blow—winds of circumstance and change, shifting, altering our lives continually.

Just as surely as that beautiful bridge crumpled and fell beneath the raging Corduroy Creek because it was built on the sand, thus will every life built on anything other than Christ the Rock falter and fall.

And great, Jesus said, would be the fall.

What about your foundation? Is your life built on the rock Christ Jesus? If not, I urge you to accept Him today as your Savior and Lord.

Begin to read His Word, the Bible; and be filled with His Spirit. Then when you face life's steady rain, when the floods come, when the winds beat upon your life, it will stand.

You will be able to sing in triumph in the midst of it all, "On Christ, the solid Rock, I stand; all other ground is sinking sand!"

Three winters and much high water have come and gone since the second real bridge was built over Corduroy Creek. This bridge has stood the test, for it is built on the rock.

'ALL THINGS' INCLUDES THE LITTLE THINGS

Romans 8:28—can you quote it? Most Christians can.

Yes, we can quote it, but how often we moan and fret, wring our hands and tear our hair about some small matter over which we have no control. The little cares nag the soul and nibble away the joy of life.

We act as if God is able to handle the calamities of life; but when it comes to little things, we have to muddle through, wondering if He really knows what's going on.

We forget that the God who made the everlasting hills also makes the gossamer snowflakes. The soon-to-melt snowflakes have their purpose. So do the little fleeting cares of our lives; they too are included in the "all things" of Romans 8:28.

This was forcibly brought home to me a few years ago by something that happened to Mamie, my coworker. We are two lady missionaries working with the Apache Indians in Arizona; and at that time our only transportation was an old van the Indians had named Nellie.

One summer afternoon Mamie (in Nellie) was on her way to Globe, Arizona, a 62-mile drive (one way) with only one small gas station along the way. She was going there to pick up a half dozen of our Indian young people who had been in camp for a week at Prescott, Arizona.

Since old Nellie would never have made the long trip to Prescott, some friends had volunteered to take our young people if we would meet them in Globe when they came back.

Nellie had given us many headaches, but we had endured, like Moses, by seeing that which was invisible; in our case a better van someday. In preparation for the trip to Globe we had taken Nellie to the garage. After a service job and thorough checkup, the mechanic thought she would make the trip.

"Anyway," I said. to Mamie, "I think everything that could happen to a single vehicle has already happened to Nellie! Almost everything on her has been repaired or replaced; surely you won't have any trouble."

Other duties made it impossible for me to go along, so Mamie had bravely set forth. She made it through the Salt River Canyon, a scenic drive of 5 miles of hairpin switchback curves down to the bottom and the same for 5 miles up the other side.

Mamie was about 15 miles beyond the canyon going down another mountain when she noticed the van losing power. The motor was running, but she was slowing down. Finally she got off the road, and the van came to a complete stop. The motor was still running, but it had no power to move.

She got out and put up the hood as a distress signal, muttering

(I am sure), "So nothing else could go wrong, huh!" Getting back into the van she asked the Lord to please send some help. It is a very lonely highway.

After awhile a highway patrolman stopped. "Having trouble, lady?" he asked politely. Mamie explained the problem.

"Hmmm. Sounds like your clutch is burned out."

"No, that can't be it; this thing is an automatic," Mamie exclaimed.

"Well, lady," he said, "in that case I don't know what it could be, but I'll have a look."

So the helpful patrolman, with Mamie peering over his shoulder, removed the air breather and began fumbling among the wires. Finally he looked up in triumph. "Here it is!" he said. "You've lost the little screw that holds this thing that connects to the gas pedal. No wonder you slowed down and stopped; you weren't getting enough gas to keep you moving. Do you happen to have a little screw?"

"I don't know," Mamie said, "but I'll take a look."

But after a thorough search of both Nellie and the patrol car, they couldn't find a thing to help them.

"Well, lady," the patrolman said, "my father-in-law lives on a ranch about 12 miles from here. I'll go over there and see what I can find. You just wait here."

"Don't worry," Mamie replied, "I'll be right here."

The time dragged. It was almost time for her to meet the young people in Globe. What would they do if she didn't get there?

Finally she saw the patrol car coming. The patrolman was smiling as he got out.

"I brought a whole handful," he said. "I sure hope one will fit."

He selected a small screw, and as Mamie watched anxiously, he tried it. Yes! It worked! The first one fit perfectly!

"How about that?" he spoke with relief. Mamie thanked him profusely and was soon on her way again.

She thanked the Lord for sending the helpful patrolman who was willing to go many extra miles, and for the tiny screw that fit perfectly. But she was still worried about the young people, for she was now nearly 2 hours late.

As she finally pulled into the parking lot in Globe where we had arranged to meet our friends, they too were just pulling into the lot!

After greeting each other, our friend said, "We had a flat tire and other delays; we were so worried that you would be here waiting and wondering what had happened to us. But the Lord timed us both just right!"

Yes, He certainly had. This was Romans 8:28 in action.

So the next time it happens to you, some little thing that promises to upset your day and scramble your plans, remember God is aware. He has no miscellaneous category marked trivia to generalize your little needs. Rather He says that yours is such an individual case that "the very hairs of your heard are all numbered" (Matthew 10:30). "All things" includes the little things, so let Him fit them into His plan for your daily life.

BESSIE'S NEW HOUSE

It was sad, in a way. I was looking at an abandoned house standing by itself in a clearing near one of the cornfields. So dilapidated. So far from town. Empty and deserted. A lonely sight.

And yet it was springtime, and new life was springing up around it.

On that particular morning, I had brought an old Apache woman up the canyon to look over the nearby cornfield. It was planting time, and the Indians on the Fort Apache Reservation were going to the fields miles up the canyon above the small village of Carrizo, where we live, to plant their corn.

Bessie wanted to go, but it was too far for her to walk. So I invited her to ride with us.

The road up the canyon is a story in itself. Rough and dusty, it climbs into the red hills following a lilting mountain stream. Graceful cottonwood trees with glistening leaves march along the dusty road.

On each side are the skeletal remains of wickiups, conical grass-thatched huts the Indian people once lived in.

Soon the red hills recede, the canyon widens, and the cornfields are in view.

It takes little imagination to put oneself back a hundred years. The scene must have been much the same then as it is today. That is why I was always a bit shocked by the sight of the old house. Why was it there? It seemed so out of place.

I was glad to have Bessie riding with us, for she is a special person. She is the embodiment of the old-time Apache women. Few of her generation are left.

Bessie always wears a camp dress with her knife in a sheath on her waist. She knows what it's like to kill a deer and tan the hide. She knows how to build a wickiup. She has built many.

She used to weave baskets; and she always made the cradleboards for her babies that were born on the dirt floor of the wickiup.

Yes, Bessie well remembers the way it used to be. She has lived to see many changes come to her people.

The greatest change, perhaps, has come with the missionaries and their gospel work. Bessie and her husband, who is now with the Lord, were among those who believed. Though old and apparently set in their Indian ways, they both found new life in Christ.

On that bright morning we stopped by the roadside, climbed through the wire fence, and made our way toward the cornfield. I went only as far as the old house, while Bessie went on.

I stood there gazing at what was left of it. Once it was a proud little residence. Now it was gray and weather-beaten. The porch sagged, the roof partly gone, the windows long since shattered.

Yet there remained a certain brave dignity, defiant of time and the elements. Like Bessie!

As I stood there wondering about the old house and the folk who once had called it home, my thoughts were interrupted by the sound of Bessie coming back. She leaned heavily on her cane as she walked, breathing hard. Poor old soul, I thought. She didn't get down to the cornfield. No doubt she realizes she won't be able to plant corn this year.

Suddenly I felt very sad for both Bessie and the house. The old woman, gray and wrinkled. The old building, gray and weather-beaten. Time and trouble had ravaged both. It was a forlorn sight.

As Bessie reached the corner of the house, she stopped. And then I noticed it! A scrawny peach tree growing by the tottering house was in full bloom. Those beautiful pink blossoms seemed to flaunt themselves in the very face of decay and death. They spoke of new life, resurrection, eternal life!

In that moment my sadness lifted. Paul's words rang in my ears: "For we know that, if our earthly house of this tabernacle were dissolved, we have a building of God, a house not made with hands, eternal in the heavens" (2 Corinthians 5:1).

True, Bessie has grown old. But one day soon she will exchange her old house for a new one. God will give her a new body, an eternal body, on the resurrection morning.

For Jesus said: "I am the resurrection, and the life: he that believeth in me, though he were dead, yet shall he live: and whosoever liveth and believeth in me shall never die. Believest thou this?" (John 11:25-26).

That's the important question. Do you believe it? Do you placed your trust in the Lord Jesus Christ? Bessie has, and though her earthly temple may perish, she will have a new house (body) eternal in the heavens.

As beautiful as the springtime blossoms on the peach tree!

DO YOU LISTEN WELL?

How is your hearing? Have you checked it recently to find out if you really hear what is said?

Do you hear what is written? When you read, do you really try to understand and act upon the helpful, worthy things the writer says?

The Bible, for instance. Does its message come through to you in a life-changing way?

Jesus put it this way: "If any man hath ears to hear, let him hear" (Mark 7:16). In fact, these words of Jesus are to be found seven times in the Gospels. They are also found as words of warning at the close of each of the messages to the seven churches in the Book of Revelation.

The Living Bible paraphrases the words this way: "If you have ears, listen!"

It is possible to hear, but not really listen. Let me tell you a story that an Indian man in Fort Hall shared with me. I think it illustrates the point very well.

My friend said it happened when he was a small boy, many years ago. He was staying with his grandfather near Fort Washakie, Wyoming. The old grandfather owned a beautiful Appaloosa horse; in fact, it was the most beautifully marked Appaloosa anyone in the area had ever seen. People often stopped to admire it.

The old man had been the proud owner of this horse for many years, but now in its old age the horse was going blind.

One day some white men came to Fort Washakie with a small traveling show. This was a great attraction, especially for the little Indian boy who had never seen some of the strange animals they had in the show.

The white men set up their show near the place where the boy and his grandfather had their teepee. The next day one of the white men came over to where the old Indian and the boy were camped.

"Hey, Chief," he yelled at the old man, "is that your horse out there?" He pointed to the beautiful Appaloosa grazing in the field.

"My horse," nodded the old man. "Well, Chief, I'll buy him.

"No, me no sell horse," said the old grandfather.

"Now, Chief, I'll give you $400 for that horse," insisted the white man.

"No, me no sell horse; horse no look good." And with those words the old Indian turned and walked into the teepee.

Later the old man asked his young grandson, "How much is $400?"

The boy told him it was enough money to buy all they needed for a long time.

"Hmmmmm," murmured the old man in deep thought.

A few days later the white men were taking down their show, preparing to leave, when the same man approached the old man and the boy again.

"Look, Chief," he said, "I really want that horse. I need him for my show. give you $500 for him, but that's my last offer!"

The old man, wrapped in his blanket, sat in silence for a long time, while the white man stood impatiently kicking the ground with his boot. Finally the old man spoke. He said, "Horse no look good."

"Aw, come on, Chief, he looks beautiful; but that's my last offer. Take it or leave it."

"OK, me sell him," said the old man.

With an air of triumph the white man counted out the money; then he walked out in the field, roped the beautiful animal, and led him away.

The old man and the boy were still camped at the same place when the same white man came riding in a few days later. But he was not riding the beautiful Appaloosa; he was leading it by a rope behind his horse.

Very angrily he jumped off his horse and stomped up to where the old Indian sat wrapped in his blanket by the fire.

"Chief," he shouted, "you beat me!"

The old man looked up in surprise. He shook his head and said, "No, me no fight; me no beat you."

"What I mean, Chief, is that this horse stumbled and fell with me. You sold me a horse that is going blind."

"Hmmmmm," replied the old Indian. "Me tell you, horse no look good!"

A humorous story, but don't blame the old Indian. He had told the white man, the best way he knew, the fault of the beautiful horse. The white man should have had "ears to hear." But his desire (greed if you will) for the horse had deafened him.

Such things as horses and money can be replaced. But spiritual things lost through carelessness, through lack of really hearing and acting upon what you hear, may be lost forever.

Have you heard God's message of love and forgiveness offered to all who will accept His Son, Jesus Christ, as Lord and Savior? Have you heard that whosoever believes on Him shall have eternal life?

Perhaps you have heard, and perhaps you can even quote some Scripture verses about it, learned long ago. But have you heard in such a way that it has changed your life? Have you acted on it? Do you know Christ or just know about Him?

The white man in the story was deafened by greed. What has

deafened you to God's message? Has it been the "attractions of this world, delights of wealth, the search for success, the lure of nice things?" (Mark 4:18, Living Bible, paraphrased).

Don't let "things" deafen you. Paul put it this way: "For the things which are seen are temporal, but the things which are not seen are eternal" (2 Corinthians 4:18). Material things will pass away. The peace of heart and mind given to those who put their trust (faith) in Christ will never pass away. The Lord gives a joy that never fades, the wonderful fact of eternal life in a perfect place.

Listen! Do you hear the gentle urging of the Holy Spirit? "Incline your ear, and come unto me; hear, and your soul shall live" (Isaiah 55:3).

Jesus told a parable of two builders. The one built his house upon the sand, and when the storms came, it collapsed. The other built on rock, and his house endured the rain and the floods that beat upon it. The wise one whose house survived, Jesus said, represents the one who hears His sayings and puts them into practice (Matthew 7:24-27).

Hear, and do. The message is clear. Will you act on the Word? Do you listen well?

END OF THE TRAIL

In the Cowboy Hall of Fame, in Oklahoma City, there is a famous bronze work by James Earl Fraser. It is his sculptural eulogy to the American Indian entitled "End of the Trail."

This sculpture has been copied many times in various art forms. In case you are not familiar with it, "End of the Trail" is an Indian wearily slumped over on his tired horse.

It seems to be a bitter reminder of all that was the glory of yesterday for the Indian. Now, the freedom of the prairies, the rivers, the lakes, and the desert that was his sovereign right is gone, forever.

We see him slumped over his weary horse, at the "end of the trail," stripped of dignity and self-respect, herded onto a reservation, an ever-dwindling piece of land. Worst of all, Fraser's work seems to picture the Indian as robbed of even the hope for the future as a people tomorrow.

But the American Indian belied Fraser's work! He did not fade into the sunset to become a romantic memory of yesteryear. The American Indian survived!

He survived neglect and poverty; he survived government policies, poor education, and poor health care. He survived even the well-meaning bureaucrats and (sorry to say) some missionaries who tried to "assimilate him" out of existence.

Yes, the American Indian survived; today nearly 1 million Indian people live among us. Most of them continue to live on the 280 reservations in the continental United States. Numerous others live in towns or in our large cities. It is reported that more than 20,000 Indians live in the Los Angeles area and 25,000 in Chicago. A few live on reservations which are state, rather than government, supervised.

But wherever he may live he is an Indian—an Indian with a heritage and a culture of which to be proud. He has not, as a people, reached the "end of the trail."

Yet there remains one aspect of "end of the trail" that is true and applicable to the Indian today. Though not vanquished as a people the Indian, like all other persons, must face the end of the trail of life itself and pass through that doorway called death.

It also is true, almost without exception, that the trail we follow all of our lives is the trail upon which we end life. What trail does the modern Indian follow? What awaits him at the end of that trail?

Heavily traveled are the trails of alcoholism and suicide. They take a grim toll of Indian people year by year. Also, in the past decade there has been a renewal of interest in Indian religion or the "Indian way." This interest is noticeable in both urban and reservation Indians. It is a trail that turns aside from the Bible and

Jesus Christ.

Of course, the Bible tells us: "There is a way that seems right to a man, but in the end it leads to death" (Proverbs 14:12, 16:25 NIV).

Jesus said: "I am the way and the truth and the life. No one comes to the Father except through me" (John 14:6 NIV).

I have had the privilege of living among and ministering to various tribes of Indian people in different areas of the country. I have found great differences in language, culture, and economic conditions; but I also have found in every place I have lived, especially among the youth, the same turning to the old way, the "Indian way."

For there is, everywhere, the same yearning for a "way," a "trail" of happiness and peace. I also have known many Indian people who have found the "Way," the "trail" of new life in Christ. I have seen the results of both trails, the right trail of life through Christ and the other trail that may have seemed right, but led to destruction.

I remember a gray March day, the bitter wind whipping my hair, as I stood by an open grave and repeated the words of the committal service for a young woman. She would surely have been alive but for the lure of the way that seemed right and the alcoholism that usually goes with that way.

A grief more bitter than the harsh March wind tore my heart that dark day when we buried Charlene. I saw her sobbing children scattered among friends and relatives, robbed of a mother by death at the end of the trail that had seemed right.

Then I think of another Indian mother and father I know. They too have a large family; they too groped their way through life on a trail of sorrow. I will let Alice and Everett Masten, from Taholah on the Quinault Reservation in Washington, tell their own story.

Alice:"Our five girls always went to Sunday school and to church. We wanted our children to know God, but we wouldn't admit that we didn't know Him. I was in awful bondage to alcohol. I wanted a better life, but how?

"I had asked the pastor (Helen Belden) and the people in the church to pray for me. Many times I thought, I am just no good; I should kill myself.

"Once when one of our boys was quite small and we were both drinking, our little boy was badly burned. It was an accident, but I felt it was my fault. I said, 'I am going to harm my children, I'll never drink again.' But about a week after he got out of the hospital I was drinking again. Oh, what a horrible, lost feeling I had!

"Then one Saturday night, when I was drinking I found myself at the door of the Bible Lighthouse Church, here in Taholah. Ordinarily they held no services on Saturday nights, but that Saturday, Sister Belden felt the Holy Spirit telling her to have one, and she obeyed!

"I went in. I went to the altar; but I was still slightly drunk when I knelt there. I am so glad they didn't turn me away because I was drinking. My girls were there. They cried and prayed for me. I know it was my daughters' prayers that brought me to the Lord!

"The next morning I felt embarrassed. Something said to me, 'Don't go back.' Other people said, 'You'll never make it.' But I went to church, and I have been coming ever since. That was in 1965. When the Lord does the work in your life, He does it well!"

Everett:"I couldn't believe that my drinking partner had left me. I said, `I'm not ever going to that church!' I had always felt I would go the way I was brought up, the Indian way, in the religion we believed. But, a few years ago I came to Jesus. He saved me and gave me new life and peace.

Brother Everett is in a wheelchair. He suffers from a deterioration of the spine, but he says: "Jesus has helped me so much in my pain, and I believe I will be completely healed someday." His peaceful spirit and radiant countenance are a wonderful testimony.

Sister Alice goes on to tell of the wonderful things God has done in every area of her life. "After I got saved I looked at my house. I had never really seen it before. We had two rooms, no curtains, hardly any furniture, no cooking stove, just a small hot plate. I said, 'Lord, I can't let my house look like this!'

"I got material and made curtains. I saw a small gas cooking stove in a store in town, I asked the clerk how much I could pay down on it; he said $20, just what I had! I was scared to tell my husband, but when I did, he didn't get angry. In a month we had paid for the entire amount and, at last, I had a real stove to cook on for our family.

"When the housing program came, we obtained a new house! I said, 'Lord, you are giving me my mansion down here!' But I had no money to buy the furniture I would need for the new house. I looked through the catalog and made a list of everything I needed. I asked the Lord to give me what was on that list. Then I put the list in my Bible and started thanking Him for my furniture.

When the house was finished, my father unexpectedly received a large sum of money. He told me to go to town and get what I needed for my house. I got everything I had written on my list, and later, a washer and dryer too!"

Brother Everett says: "We were just like any other Indian family; we were in sin and bound by drink, but Jesus saved us."

Today seven of the eight Masten children are saved. The youngest girl, Alena, is a student at the Good Shepherd (Indian) Bible School in Mobridge, South Dakota. The Mastens are a family closely knit together in the love that only Jesus Christ can give.

I remember hearing another Indian woman in the Northwest say one evening, as she and her husband were preparing to leave at the close of a visit, "It's time to cut trails for home."

When I think of the many Indian people walking on the trail that will end in death, my heart cries out, Isn't it time we cut trails, toward the trail that leads home to heaven, for Indian people?

If we (every Christian who reads this) would pray fervently for revival among American Indians what a mighty trail toward God, for Indian people, we could cut.

If we would pray faithfully for Indian ministers to be thrust into the harvest and for support to come in for those Indians who are now struggling to work among their own people, a great trail could be cut to lead Indians to the Lord.

If we would pray earnestly for and support our Indian Bible schools, an effective trail to change Indian lives quickly could be cut!

Which trail will it be for the Indian people? The trail of new life in Christ or the old trail of death? How many families like the Mastens are out there waiting? Will we see them find life, or will we bury them one by one in bitter sorrow?

Yes, the "end of the trail" of life is coming for every American Indian. God grant it will not be depicted by a weary, defeated brave, but by a triumphant Christian Indian!

'HOLD ONTO THE BOOK'

For centuries the Hopi Indians, known as the peaceful ones, have lived near or atop the mesas that lie scattered across the Colorado River plateau like jumbled pieces of a giant jigsaw puzzle. Their villages blend so well with the rock on which they are built that the unobservant could easily miss seeing them.

But not all Hopi live on their reservation. Some in search of employment have moved to nearby towns like Winslow, which has a sizable Indian population. Hopi, Navajo, Pueblo, and other tribes people can be found here.

Our church, the Indian Assembly of God in Winslow, has Indians from several tribes; but we all belong to the same family, the family of God!

During Wednesday night Bible study recently we were talking about the importance of the Word of God, and one of the Hopi women told us the following story:

I remember what my grandfather used to tell me. When we

were small, we had to sit down every night and listen to his stories. Grandfather would often say: 'If you ever get a hold of the black book, never let go of it. Always hold onto the book.'

My grandfather was not a Christian, and I didn't know what he meant. It made no sense to me. I don't know how the old people knew about the black book.

Years later when I got saved, one of my old uncles said: 'Now you have found the black book; hold onto it.'

Only then did I realize that this Bible [she raised her Bible, tears in her eyes] is the Book my grandfather was talking about.

Other Hopi people in the congregation were nodding their heads. Yes, they agreed, they too had been told to hold onto the Book.

I was amazed to hear this, for the Hopi are the most traditional of Indians, having retained more of the religious and social practices of their ancestors than any other Arizona tribe.

But the power of "the Book" had made itself known. How? I wondered.

Perhaps a godly Catholic priest had implanted a reverence for the "black Book." (The Catholics sent missionaries to the Hopi as early as 1628.) Or could it have been one of the Mennonite missionaries who came later and labored long among the Hopi? Maybe it was something a Christian teacher in a boarding school planted in the heart of a young Hopi.

However it came, the message had been passed down from old to young for years: "Hold onto the Book."

The tragedy is that these people did not know the teaching that was in the Book they respected. They never knew the truth about Jesus Christ, the One revealed in the Book. They never learned that He could change their lives. The black Book was only a mysterious thing that had some power they did not understand.

I am glad there are many Indian people today who not only reverence the Book but understand the wonderful gospel it contains. They have read the Book and learned about Jesus Christ who lived and died and rose again that they might live eternally.

They love to quote John 3:16: "For God so loved the world, that he gave his only begotten Son, that whosoever believeth in him should not perish, but have everlasting life."

So many people have wished they could wipe out the past and start over. The Book tells them they can. Everyone may have another chance, a new beginning, for it says: "Therefore if any man be in Christ, he is a new creature: old things are passed away; behold all things are become new" (2 Corinthians 5:17).

Our Indian people at Winslow have learned to hold onto the Book when the fears and troubles of life come sweeping over them. They love to read Psalm 56:3-4 which says: "What time I am afraid, I will trust in thee. In God I will praise his word, in God I have put my trust; I will not fear what flesh can do unto me."

One of their favorite verses is Hebrews 13:8 which says: "Jesus Christ the same yesterday, and today, and for ever." This assures them they have a Friend whose love and care for them never changes.

When tempted to worry over financial problems or future security, they like to turn to Scripture verses like Philippians 4:19 which says: "My God shall supply all your need according to his riches in glory by Christ Jesus."

When they are lonely or tempted to do wrong, they have learned to open the Book and read about the One who understands their temptation and who is able to sustain them. They find that "the Lord knoweth how to deliver the godly out of temptations" (2 Peter 2:9).

They remember the old grandfather's admonition, "Hold onto the book." They do not leave it on a shelf gathering dust, but open its pages, and it gives them hope, faith, and instruction for Christian living.

I HEAR A CRY

The Fort Apache Reservation in Arizona boasts many scenic splendors. Come with me for a visit to one of these places, the Salt Banks, where we will see a panorama of strange, startling beauty.

In the bottom of Salt River Canyon we turn off Highway 60 and travel (at your own risk, the sign says) a rough, narrow road. The scenery is breathtaking along this winding road which clings to the cliffs above the mighty Salt River.

About seven miles later we park our truck, for the remainder of the trip must be made on foot. As we walk along a steep trail, far ahead we see dazzling white cliffs sparkling in the sunlight—a sharp contrast to the blue-green water of the river and the rugged, red mountains surrounding us.

As we come closer, the brilliant cliffs take on the appearance of ocean waves cresting in midair. Now we see many unusual formations all sculptured in glistening white. Let your imagination go, and the formations become castles, animals, and science-fiction or fairytale creatures molded in sparkling white salt.

The Salt Banks extend along the river for nearly a mile. This is one of the largest salt deposits in Arizona. A pure saline solution from salt water springs drips from the banks, forming tiny delicate tubes of damp salt. You may break them off, but be careful, since they are fragile. Much of the area is cave-like, and the stalactites are formed of pure salt.

As a center of many religious beliefs and legends, the Salt Banks have long been important to the Apache people. As we stand gazing in wonder, I will tell you a story several different Apache people told me. There are variations, some quite involved.

Long ago many people lived here under these hills, by this river. Then one day the water became too salty for drinking or cooking. The people decided to move away.

One of the families in the rush and sorrow of moving forgot a basket. Baskets were very important; in fact, so much so, they sent a little girl back to look for it. Her little dog followed her.

The little girl got lost and sat down and cried and cried. Her tears turned to salt, and the little dog barked and howled sadly as it tried to find her.

Some people say that even today, if you come to these Salt Banks, climb into one of the caves, and sit quietly, perhaps you will hear the little dog barking or the little Indian maiden crying.

Yes, come to the Salt Banks, climb into the weird caves, sit quietly, listen carefully. Perhaps you too will hear a cry.

I have heard it. It is not a cry one hears with the ears but rather with the heart—not the cry of one little lost Indian maiden but the cries of a proud and valiant people, the American Indians.

Hear the heartbreaking cry of a people who through tremendous effort have made themselves a significant part of the 20th century. They have done so with the help of both government and churches. Yet often it has been this very help they had to overcome; for what was supposed to have been help consisted of demeaning programs, bent on keeping Indian people dependent, second-class citizens.

Listen to the cry of a people struggling against overwhelming odds of disease, poverty, and the ever-present frustration these bring. Some seeking an escape from it all have turned to alcohol, but it has no answer for the cry of the heart.

Can't you hear the cry of the Indian people seeking in their ancient ceremonies the answers to age-old questions of life and death?

In Acts 16:9 we read that Paul had a vision of a man from Macedonia who wanted help. I have a vision. It is of the American Indians. Like the man in Paul's vision, they too are crying out for help.

There was only one way Paul could help the people of Macedonia —by going and preaching the gospel to them. He had to tell them about Jesus, for Jesus alone was the answer to their need. Even so, the gospel is the only answer to the American Indian's need.

In John 7:37 we read that Jesus offered the water of life to any who would come unto Him. The Indians of America need to respond to Christ's invitation; they need to call out to Him.

But Romans 10:14-15 asks these questions: "How then shall they call on him in whom they have not believed? and how shall they believe in him of whom they have not heard? and how shall they hear without a preacher? and how shall they preach, except they be sent? as it is written, How beautiful are the feet of them that preach the gospel of peace, and bring glad tidings of good things!"

You, through prayer, can help answer these questions. Begin today to pray that the Lord of the harvest will send forth laborers, Indian men and women to preach the gospel.

Pray for our Indian Bible institutes and for the few (compared to the great need) who have been graduated from these schools and are striving to reach their own people.

Pray for an outpouring of the Holy Spirit on every Indian tribe in America. I didn't say "every reservation," for many Indians have lost their lands. Many others have left their reservations, but all retain their tribal identity.

Yes, I hear a cry, a far sadder cry than that of the little lost girl in the legend of the Salt Banks. It is a cry from the hearts of living men and women, hundreds of thousands of American Indians.

I hear a cry. Do you?

'JESUS MUST BE REAL'

Would Helen try to settle matters according to the Apache way? I knew it called for vengeance!

Apache Indian customs and the teaching of Jesus Christ are often as far apart as east and west. What happens when Christianity and Indian culture clash?

Of course, some of the customs that comprise the Apache way of life are excellent and compatible with Christianity—such as the belief in sharing with your relatives or friends in need.

But there are other Apache customs that can bring fear and bloodshed. Here's an example:

In the case of murder or serious bodily injury, the relatives of the victim feel they have the right to avenge the crime by killing either the guilty person or one of his close relatives.

A hundred years of the white man's law has not done completely away with this type of thinking. I know, for I have lived on the Fort Apache Reservation as a missionary for a number of years. I have known Apache people to live in fear for months after someone in their family committed a serious crime. With good reason they feared the relatives of the victim.

What effect does the gospel of Jesus Christ have on this ingrained way of thinking? Can age-old customs of vengeance be changed to love and forgiveness? Can what Paul wrote to the

Corinthians apply also to the Apache? "Therefore if any man be in Christ, he is a new creature; old things are passed away; behold all things are become new," 2 Corinthians 5:17 tells us.

I will tell you the story of Helen, an Apache woman. Then judge for yourself the power of Christ today in the lives of Apache people.

Helen is a Christian. Several years ago she and her husband William accepted the Lord.

When she became a Christian, she had only one living son, having lost her other children at birth or shortly thereafter. She prayed for children, and God answered. In the course of time she had two boys and a girl.

Though these children were greatly loved, it was Delbert, her oldest son, who was the "apple of her eye." Delbert was a quiet boy, and in obedience to his parents' wishes he finished high school when most others his age were dropouts. Occasionally Delbert attended church, but he showed no interest in becoming a Christian.

Delbert had been out of school several months. Jobs were hard to find on the reservation, and he had not found steady work. That was why he was out riding his horse one bright, fall day and decided to ride the few miles up the highway to the tribally owned store. This little gas station carries a few groceries, but its big sale items are wine and beer.

That day when I answered the phone, the man's voice on the line was shaking. He spoke rapidly, "Sister Jo Ann? Is this Sister Jo Ann?"

"Yes, it is," I said. "Who is this? What's wrong?"

"Get Helen and come up here to the junction (the place where the tribal store is located). Delbert has been shot; come quick." He hung up. I stood staring at the phone, almost unable to believe the message.

My co-worker volunteered to take our church van and go up into the mountains where Delbert's father was working to bring him back. I ran to my car to go get Helen.

When I found her, I gave her the message as we sped up the highway. She never said a word, but the look of sorrow and fear on her face almost broke my heart. Then she began to pray in a whisper, "Jesus, Jesus; help me, Jesus."

We got to the little store, and I vividly remember the quiet group of Indian men standing in a nearby field. We ran to them, and they parted silently to let us through. Delbert, unconscious, lay on the ground, writhing in agony.

I saw the gaping hole in his upper thigh. I felt my knees get weak, and my stomach begin to churn. His clothes and the ground were soaked with blood. I had never seen so much blood, and it continued to spurt out of the ragged, awful wound.

A state policeman was standing there. I asked him if he had a first-aid kit. He went back to his car and returned with one.

A young Apache man, a close relative to Delbert, began to help me as I tore into the first-aid box. I hastily opened packages of bandages, making a compress of them. I told my helper to put them into the hole where the blood was spurting out. "Push them down hard," I instructed him, and he quickly obeyed.

We packed the terrible wound and wrapped and tied strips of bandage around the leg. The flow of blood seemed to be stemmed.

All this time Helen was on her knees, Delbert's head cradled in her arms. The tears streamed down her cheeks as she quietly prayed and talked to Delbert.

"What happened? Who did this?" I asked.

In a trembling voice the young man helping me named a man from our village. "He thought it was me," the young man said. He went on to explain: "That man is mad at me. He came up here with a rifle and said he was going deer hunting; but he got drunk. When he saw Delbert out here on his horse, he thought it was me, and he shot him with the rifle. He meant to kill."

"We have him down there in that pickup," he continued, nodding toward a nearby truck. "The police will take him in, and we called the ambulance."

I knew it was 30 miles to the hospital. The ambulance had a long way to come. Then I noticed Helen was gone.

"Where is Helen?" I asked. There was no spoken reply. Someone just pointed a finger toward the pickup where the man who had tried to kill Delbert was sitting.

I got to my feet and started toward the truck, my thoughts in a turmoil.

I knew the "Apache way." Would Helen try to settle matters right here, or would she only make threats? I knew that according to the Apache way, this would call for vengeance.

When I reached the truck, I saw the guard had opened the door. The would-be murderer sat in a drunken stupor; Helen was talking. Apache (to my ears, at least) is an abrupt language. When spoken in anger, the sound of the words seems to cut and burn the air.

But Helen was not speaking in anger. She manifested no hatred or bitterness in either countenance or voice.

When she saw me, she switched to English, speaking in the same gentle voice, choked with tears.

"I told him," she said, "this is what sin does; this is what drinking and getting mad does. If you knew Jesus, you would not be like this—you would never do this. Jesus is the One who helps me to forgive you. We will pray for you."

I stood in speechless amazement at this demonstration of the power of Christ at work in this woman's life. We did pray for the drunken man and also for Delbert.

Finally the ambulance came. Helen went with Delbert to the hospital. It was a long ordeal for Delbert. He spent many weeks on his back in bed, but he did not lose his leg.

The story doesn't end there. This case could have been taken to federal court in Tucson. But Helen and her husband refused to press charges. So the guilty man served a 100-day sentence in the reservation jail.

Helen and her husband had no way to travel, so they asked me to take them to visit the man while he was in jail. I gladly did so. When we arrived at the jail and they brought the man into the visitation area, he stepped back in fear when he saw his visitors.

They quickly assured him they had come only to pray for him and to tell him, now that he was sober, that they forgave him.

Looking at me the man said, "I know Jesus must be real because I know if I were these people and someone did to my son what I did to theirs, I would hate him. I might even try to kill him."

What a tremendous testimony this incident is to the transforming power of the gospel!

It also changed the victim's life. Delbert is now married. Both he and his wife are Christians and both teach Sunday school. He testifies that it was the Lord who saved his life, his leg, and above all, his soul.

LIVING WATER

One far-off yesterday a woman carrying her water jug came to a well. She intended to fill the jug with water as she had done countless times before.

That day a man was sitting by the well. He started a conversation, first asking her for a drink of water. Then He told her about the water that quenches the thirst of the human soul, living water.

The woman listened, intently, for hers was a thirsty heart. She knew well the unquenchable thirst of loneliness, guilt, depression, fear—they all were part of her life; nothing satisfied their demands. Nothing, that is, until that day, the day she met a man called Jesus who gave her water that was not in the well, living water! (You may read this story in detail in the Gospel of John, chapter 4.)

But centuries have come and gone since that day. Is Jesus still the same? Can His message relate to people of a far different age, a people caught in a struggle between two cultures? Can He satisfy the thirst of their hearts? Does the living water still have its power?

Let me share a story. I am a missionary to the American Indians, and I know well the "old woman" in this story.

The sun was high in the sky now, and it was warm, very warm for early spring. The old Indian woman, her arms loaded with shoots from the mulberry bushes, stood gazing at the red hills.

She felt so tired. How long had she been here cutting these things? A long time surely, for she had risen to boil her coffee over the small fire she built outside under the brush shade before the sun came out of its resting place. That was so much better, being out in the air in an open place, rather than being shut inside the house—the white man's kind of house she lived in now.

After drinking a big tin cup of black coffee with much sugar in it and eating a tortilla left from yesterday, she prepared her lunch—some jerky and the rest of the tortillas folded together and carefully wrapped in newspaper someone had left under the shade.

She placed the lunch and a large knife in the middle of her blanket. The corners she tied loosely. Then putting it over her head she let it hang across her shoulders. The woman would carry her load of mulberry shoots home in the blanket in the same way.

Picking up her heavy walking stick she started up the canyon just as dawn broke all pink and silver across the gray eastern sky.

Now the sun was high overhead. "Time to eat my lunch," she said half aloud, and she began to walk back to the place on the bank of the creek where she had left her lunch wrapped in the blanket.

Kneeling by the creek she washed her hands. Then she took a long drink, scooping up the water in her hands until her thirst was quenched. When she finished drinking, she splashed the cool water over her head and face.

With a few deft motions the Indian woman brushed the twigs aside and sat down on the ground, smoothing the long, full skirt of her dress around her. She untied the blanket and took out her lunch. Holding the tortilla and jerky in her wrinkled brown hands she looked up at the bright blue sky, smiled, and murmured her thanks.

Slowly she ate her lunch. She sat gazing at the quiet stream of water which had flowed for so many years through these red hills. It had been cutting the valley through the hills, home to her people, longer than anyone could remember. Sunlight and shadow played over the surface of the creek. Ah, it looks and sounds almost alive, the woman thought, and in a way it is because it is the same creek I remember as a young girl.

She smiled as she thought of how she used to run to the creek and jump into its clear, cool water every morning, even winter mornings! Then her clothing would be frozen stiff and icicles would be hanging in her long hair, making a sound like bells as she ran back to the wickiup.

Yes, the same creek is still flowing as it did when we knelt by it to fill our tus. She picked up some of the mulberry shoots she had cut and looked at them carefully. They would be good for weaving; but the tus she would weave with them and coat with pitch inside and outside would never be used as a water jug. No, someone who just wanted a tus to keep to remember the old days would buy it, she hoped.

Ah, the old days when this creek that seems almost alive meant so much to our people, the woman reminisced. We always lived near its water; it satisfied the thirst of our bodies. But many were the ceremonies we held by its banks trying to satisfy the thirst of our hearts.

She stared at the creek, but her eyes were seeing far away into yesterday.

The old Indian woman thought of those ceremonies, those old days; she thought of her father and mother now gone. There were good times, she recalled, when we had enough food and clothing, but the bad times always came.

She thought of the fear that gripped her heart when troubles came—when, perhaps, someone had put a spell on them. The only answer, of course, was to seek out the medicine man. His services never were cheap. With his help sometimes horses were found, or the sick one got well; but often, oh so often, there was only loss, death, fear, and loneliness—always the questions you could not ask.

The old woman nodded as she watched the sparkling water of the creek. Yes, we had a longing, a thirst that this water could not satisfy; we had questions the ceremonies could not answer, she mused.

Then she thought of the day the missionaries came to the village. Her people had seen missionaries before, of course, at the boarding school and when they came once in a while through the village and gave out the black books and talked about their religion. But who needed the white man's religion? We had our own. She smiled as she remembered.

These missionaries, however, were different. They built a house and stayed in the village. They did not talk about religion—they talked about someone named Jesus.

Her parents were quite old when they heard the story about Jesus, for she herself was already grown and married. Her parents believed the story. Then she believed it.

So many of her people became Christians. Now they had no fear of spells. They no longer needed the services of the medicine man, for Jesus had all power, and He protected them from evil.

Death no longer was something they could not mention. The missionary told them how Jesus had defeated death. Because He is alive, they could be resurrected or caught up to Christ to live forever!

Best of all, there was no more thirst which nothing satisfied. Because Jesus' presence and peace filled the heart, the emptiness and loneliness were dispelled.

A sudden gust of wind shook the branches of the trees and ruffled the waters of the creek. Its coolness startled the woman, and she shook herself out of her memories. "I must hurry," she said aloud. "I need to get back down the canyon so I can rest before time for the church service tonight."

She got up, dusted off her skirt, piled the mulberry shoots in the blanket, tied the blanket corners together, and put the bundle on her back.

Bent under the weight of her load, she leaned heavily on her walking stick as she started toward the road. Then she stopped and turned to look again at the creek. Her weathered, brown face broke into a happy smile.

"Yes, little creek," she said, "you do seem almost alive, and you did satisfy our thirst as best you could. But now we know about Jesus. He is alive, and He gives us living water!"

MAINTAIN YOUR SPEED

While I was driving through a long tunnel, my attention was attracted by flashing red signs overhead that insistently repeated: "Maintain Your Speed." A tunnel is no place to slow down!

Those signs started me thinking about the tunnel like experiences we often pass through in life. What happens when you find yourself in a dim tunnel?

Perhaps it is a tunnel of disappointment, shattered dreams, broken promises. Maybe it is a time of failure, and you wonder if you ever will walk in sunlight again.

Some are living through the aftermath of tragedy or the death of a loved one—times so similar to groping your way through a gloom-filled tunnel.

Or perhaps the daily grind is getting to you. The countless demands seem to have no real purpose. You work hard but see little accomplished. This too can become like an unending tunnel growing darker and darker.

The message in the flashing lights can apply to whatever tunnel you find yourself stumbling through: — "Maintain Your Speed." Don't slow down. Don't become a dropout from life.

But how? How do I find meaning in life? In the midst of a tunnel how do I maintain my speed?

To find the answers to these legitimate questions, you must first of all determine the direction you are traveling. Because you have lost perspective, you may be traveling in circles. "There is a way which seemeth right unto a man; but the end thereof are the ways of death" (Proverbs 14:12).

But Jesus Christ said: "I am the way, the truth, and the life: no man cometh unto the Father, but by me" (John 14:6).

He also said: "Him that cometh to me I will in no wise cast out" (John 6:37).

So first of all, accept Christ as the way—the way to live abundantly and eternally (John 10). "And this is life eternal, that they might know thee the only true God, and Jesus Christ, whom thou hast sent" (John 17:3).

Come to Him; commit your life right where you are, just the way you are, to Him. Ask Him to be your Guide through the tunnels of life. He is still the same Jesus we read about in the Bible: "Jesus Christ the same yesterday, and today, and for ever" (Hebrews 13:8).

Realize the wonderful truth that you will never walk alone

through a tunnel experience, for He said: "I will never leave thee, nor forsake thee. So that we may boldly say, The Lord is my helper, and I will not fear what man shall do unto me" (Hebrews 13:5-6).

After you have come to Him and have accepted Him as your Lord, you can "maintain your speed," your walk of faith, by asking Him to help you turn aside from any things in your life (attitudes, actions, habits) that hinder you in your walk with Him. Perhaps some of these things contribute to the tunnels you are going through!

You continue to "maintain your speed" as you learn the language of praise and the power of prayer. You learn these by reading the Bible and walking in its light and direction.

The psalmist David said: "I will bless the Lord at all times: his praise shall continually be in my mouth" (Psalm 34:1).

In many other places throughout the Bible we read the language of praise. Learn it; speak it every day. Ask Jesus to put the language of praise in your heart, for out of the heart the mouth speaks!

But to "maintain your speed" consistently you need prayer as well as praise. In fact, the language of sincere praise should flow naturally from fervent prayer. Together they build the forward momentum of faith—secure trust in Him and in His Word.

"Be careful for nothing; but in everything by prayer and supplication with thanksgiving let your requests be made known unto God" (Philippians 4:6). That shows the relation between prayer and praise; it is an excellent verse to remember to help you "maintain your speed."

Even after you have come to Him and know you are traveling in the right direction, walk with Him. There will be times when the storms of life will beat upon you and you will feel as if you are in a dark tunnel with no end in sight. But in those times remember your hand is in His nail-scarred hand. He has already walked through every tunnel you will ever face.

"For we have not a high priest which cannot be touched with the feeling of our infirmities; but was in all points tempted like as we are, yet without sin. Let us therefore come boldly unto the throne of grace, that we may obtain mercy, and find grace to help in time of need" (Hebrews 4:15-16).

So learn to wait upon Him in prayer; offer praise in whatever tunnel you are going through. "In every thing give thanks: for this is the will of God in Christ Jesus concerning you" (1 Thessalonians 5:18). Let praise flow from your heart.

Remember tunnels do end in sunlight when you walk through life with Jesus. But in the meantime, remember also the sign in the flashing lights: "Maintain Your Speed!"

NEVER ALONE AT CHRISTMAS

The little Indian girl Willena, her dark eyes shining with excitement, ran toward my car that cold December morning. I was there to transport her to Sunday school. Since usually she was a quiet, shy child, I wondered why she was fairly bubbling over that morning.

"Church Lady!" she called out, as she approached the car. My name was difficult for some of the children to remember, so they solved the problem in a simple way; I was "Church Lady."

"Church Lady," she repeated, "my grandfather wants to see you. Come to the house."

A panoramic review of my only contact with Willena's grandfather flashed through my mind. I met him when an Indian lady, Julia Coby, and I had visited the family. I remembered his silence and his direct, rather calculating, stare. My feeling was that I was being weighed in the balance of Indian evaluation. It left me wondering if I was "found wanting. Slowly I moved from the car.

"Hurry, Church Lady," Willena called.

Both grandfather and grandmother were waiting. They motioned toward the couch. I sat down. We exchanged a few words about the weather—a safe topic anywhere.

There was silence. I waited. Grandfather cleared his throat and began to tell me about the annual Christmas celebrations held in the community meetinghouses (called lodges) scattered across the reservation.

I nodded, still silent. I had learned earlier—in Apacheland—that most white people talk too much. So I sat listening as though I had nothing else to do, but realizing all the time I was behind schedule.

Grandfather continued describing the way Christmas would be observed. There would be treats for everyone and small gifts for the children.

As I listened, I was trying to think of why he might be giving me this information. What did he want of me?

Then he paused, gave that penetrating look I remembered so well, and asked, "Would you bring your church Christmas program out to our lodge—the Eagle Lodge—and put the program on for us?"

I nearly fell off the couch! That was the last thing I expected!

Before I could reply, he continued, "A long time ago when Jack Bennett* was here, he would have a Christmas program at the lodge for us. I am one of those in charge at Eagle Lodge, and I am inviting you to bring your people and have a Christmas program for us."

Carefully I told him how glad I was to learn of how Christmas was celebrated at the lodge. It was nice too, I indicated, that treats and gifts were given.

Then, coming to the question, I said I felt honored he wanted us to put on our Christmas program at the lodge. I would ask the people at the church how they felt about it. I was certain; however, they would be happy to come.

"We want you to come on Christmas Eve. That is when we give out our treats and gifts," he specified.

Christmas Eve! That was on Sunday night—the night we planned to have our program at the church.

I wondered how the Indian Christians would react to being asked to give up a warm, comfortable church for an old, undoubtedly drafty building on the reservation.

My misgivings were not voiced. When I brought Willena home from church, I would give the decision, I told him.

I should have known better than to doubt the willingness of our people to sacrifice. These wonderful Indian people of the Fort Hall Assembly of God were a dedicated group. Eagerly they responded to the invitation, noting many years had passed since they had received such an invitation. So we began to make plans to take our program to Eagle Lodge.

Though happy for the invitation, I realized I was a newcomer to Fort Hall. How would I be received by the Indian people who would be there the night of the program?

How could I manage it all? The couple who worked with me were making plans to return to the East for a Christmas vacation. I would be alone with the responsibility, a stranger in a strange place indeed on Christmas Eve!

Our program would consist of the usual recitations and songs by the younger children. For the older classes, I prepared an uncomplicated drama to be pantomimed, interspersed with familiar carols by a small choir.

Our practice sessions went the way practice sessions usually go—some could make it for one practice, others for the next. At first all the boys wanted to be shepherds and all the girls just had to be angels.

Slowly it began to take shape. We decided to have the church program and gifts on Saturday night. On Sunday night we would all go to Eagle Lodge.

Secretly I still was worried. I reminded the Lord of all I had to do and of how alone I was.

A young couple, Dave and Zelberta Begay, called me aside and asked, "Sister Craver, how will you pick up all the people by yourself? How will you get all the articles needed and the children out to Eagle Lodge?"

"I need help," I told them. "Would you be able to help me?"

"Yes, we will help you," Zelberta said. "Dave will pick up the people for you on Saturday night. We also will pick them up for Sunday school. On Sunday night we will help you take everything and everyone out to the lodge. Dave will drive the church car. I will take a load in our pickup. It has a camper on it."

"Wonderful!" I replied.

At the next practice one of the teenage girls said, "Sister Craver, don't worry about white towels. I'll bring some extra towels for those without a towel."

I had asked each member of the choir to wear a white towel with a red, crepe-paper bow for a choir cape. My plan was to supply the bows but I would be short on towels. Karalee's offer was another load lifted.

The following Sunday, Sister Pearl Barngrover, who drove many miles each Sunday to help us, said, "Sister Craver, I will be here Saturday night to play for the program." She knew I did not play the piano. Then she volunteered to take her little electric organ to Eagle Lodge.

Julia Coby, a faithful Indian Christian, said, "My husband and I and our young people will clean. the church after the program Saturday night. We will get it ready for Sunday school."

By that time I was beginning to feel better. I could even ask the Lord at that point to forgive my secret worries. True, a stranger I still would be at Eagle Lodge, but certainly I was not going to have to make the Christmas presentation alone.

So we went to Eagle Lodge. We took the manger, the robes, the Wise Men's crowns, the odds and ends. By the time I had all the property packed, I felt as though I had a traveling show. Even so, I kept wondering if I was leaving something behind.

Eagle Lodge was cold. Several wood-burning stoves were blazing furiously, but they could not begin to warm the big, old building.

"Hey, Sister Craver, where are the towels and bows?" someone yelled. Only a few towels were on hand.

"Aren't they in that box?" I questioned.

"Nope."

"Well," I murmured, "guess what we forgot?"

"Oh, well, we can sing without them!" was the jaunty answer.

By 7 o'clock nearly all the wooden bleacher-type benches were filled with Indian people. The big building was circular, so our audience surrounded us on every side. With the manger placed on center floor, a chair on each side for Mary and Joseph, and with Sister Barngrover and her little organ to one side, we were ready to .raise the imaginary curtains.

Willena's grandfather stepped forward and told the crowd who we were. He had invited us to put on a Christmas program, he said. I thought I could detect a bit of a challenge in his voice. He nodded toward me, and I went forward.

I mentioned we were glad for the invitation to share our Christmas program and announced I was going to open the program with prayer.

Immediately a hush came over the crowd. After prayer, I asked the audience to join us in a song. Together we sang the familiar words of "Silent Night! Holy Night!" As we sang, I seemed to feel a miraculous joy of Christmas begin to flow through the drafty old building.

Smaller children gave their recitations and sang their songs. As the children who made up the choir came forward, some of the church adults stepped forward also, indicating they would help sing. With my grateful approval, others joined them until all the church adults, including the men, were part of the choir. It was a minor miracle brought about, I felt, by the warm, wonderful presence of the Holy Spirit that was permeating the building.

As I listened to the choir sing, I realized I had spoken truth in my opening remark—I was glad to be there! I was glad for each child who was doing so well in our crude setting; glad for those who so willingly were helping me bear the responsibility; glad for the men and women who had stepped forward to join the choir; and especially glad for our message and the response it was bringing.

The narrator had come to words: "So Jesus was born that long ago night, born to a lonely couple far from their home. He was born in a strange place, among strangers. 'He came unto his own, and his own received him not. But as many as received him, to them gave he power to become the sons of God.'

I was reminded that Jesus understood what it is like to be a stranger. I looked at the people—strangers to me—seated on the hard benches. They were watching the program intently. Many emotions were mirrored in the brown faces.

As I continued to look across the crowd, I suddenly realized they were not all strangers to me.

Eyes met mine and lighted with smiles of recognition. I could not recall all the names, but I knew I had visited those individuals, and those; yes, those over there too. That older man who was smiling at me; where had I met him? Oh, yes; at the jail service. "Jesus, meet the need of his heart," I found myself praying.

When our program ended, a woman stepped forward to make a short speech. She thanked us for coming. She went on to say that for too long the people had met there on Christmas Eve without really thinking about what Christmas meant. "But you have shown us what up with Christmas really means. This is the way it should be," she said, "and we hope you will come back next year."

Then someone came to me and thrust a small package into my hands. "This is for you from our committee," I was told.

Every eye in the building was on me as I unwrapped the gift. Inside I found an exquisite piece of beadwork. It was a barrette—the most beautiful imaginable! My eyes were misty as I thanked the Eagle Lodge committee for the lovely gift.

Never will I have enough hair to wear that beautiful barrette, but I shall keep it—a treasured gift! It will remind me that Jesus, whose birth we honor at Christmas, never leaves us alone. Others become His hand extended to help us carry out our responsibilities on earth. Because of Him, strangers become friends. And because of Christmas, I am part of a blessed family—a family that encompasses all races. For as many as receive Him "become the children of God" .(John 1:12 Amplified).

NO LONGER A STRANGER

Christmas in an Indian church on the reservation is much like Christmas anywhere—the programs, the recitations, the last-minute hassles. Someone doesn't show up; someone forgets the long-rehearsed lines; the angel forgets to throw away her gum!

We have a tree, cut by one of the Indian men and lovingly decorated by all the people. There are quilts and presents—dolls, cars, books—sent by thoughtful Women's Missionary Council groups. The Indian people bring presents for the two lady missionaries.

Last year's Christmas began much the same as usual. After the program was over, we took the people home, and the Indian couple responsible for the janitorial work swept and tidied the church. The two of us went into the house, exhausted and happy yet a little sad. Tomorrow would be Christmas Day, and we hadn't had time to bake or prepare anything for ourselves.

We were quiet the next morning. We felt rather alone as we opened gifts sent by WMCs and our families. Suddenly we realized just how far away our loved ones were. Though we were still within the borders of the United States, we realized we were strangers in a strange land, alone at Christmastime.

"Well, what shall we do?" we asked each other, already knowing the answer. We would go to the cafe in town and eat our Christmas dinner, just as in years past. The prospect was not too cheerful.

We were dressed and ready for the long drive into town when we heard a soft knock at the door. We opened it to find standing there the little Indian girl from the house on the hill above us.

Her smile radiant, her eyes sparkling, she announced, "My mother says for you two to come eat dinner with us, please. And hurry."

She was already running back up the hill as I stammered, "Yes, yes; we'll come."

The house on the hill, with its two tiny rooms, is home for Charlene Cody and her six small children.

Her husband deserted her and now she struggles to raise her family alone. Her only assistance is a meager welfare check. Though our small community offers both running water and electricity, she cannot afford either of these benefits.

A few months before, Mrs. Cody had started coming to church. She soon accepted the Lord and was filled with the Holy Spirit. Now she was showing God's love by sharing her Christmas dinner with us.

When we started up the hill, to our great surprise we saw more people coming in the same direction. When we entered the house, which was scrubbed spotless, we were further amazed.

Set buffet-style on a long bench was Christmas dinner—turkey and dressing, yams, gravy, vegetables, salad, hot rolls, and dessert. The older children helped serve. Their joy at being able to share was beautiful to see. There was room for only a few to be seated at the small table, so others found seats on the beds, on the floor, or outside.

Thirty-two people ate dinner there that day. Many of them, like us, would have had nothing special for Christmas if it had not been for this family who sacrificed their time and money on behalf of others.

As we bowed our heads to give thanks for the food, I realized I no longer felt alone. Although the people around me were of a different race and culture and were speaking a different language, I no longer felt like a stranger. It was the happiest Christmas I ever had!

This little story doesn't need to end here. You can add to it. Some lonely person lives near you. Why not do something special for that one this Christmas? Share your home and your Christmas dinner. Most of all, share the Christ of Christmas.

REMEMBERING AT CHRISTMAS

The best things in life are free!" An old cliché. To me some of the "best things in life" are memories I have of "little things"—such as Mother's smile at my childhood triumphs. I can't remember all of the hurdles I overcame, but I remember the love in her smile.

Many other little memories, especially of Christmas, bring me joy.

The smell of pine reminds me of the excitement of trimming the tree, hiding presents, and a myriad of other activities associated with what Christmas means to most of us. For Christmas above every other event of the year is filled with memories.

Now I am a missionary to the Apache Indians and live in a small, rather isolated Apache community. Having spent a number of Christmas seasons here, my life has been enriched with many happy memories of little things that have happened during these years.

For instance, I recall such seemingly insignificant events as children saying their recitations in the Christmas program, their clear voices singing "Joy to the World"... the presents, with our names on them so carefully wrapped, under the church tree... little children at the door saying, "We got something for you!" and proudly handing us a cake "our mother made."

Going to look for a Christmas tree with an Apache family and not finding one we liked... having the truck get stuck and spotting the perfect tree as we struggle, push, and laugh... being invited to eat dinner with a family who shared all they had to provide Christmas dinner for others.

I remember the couple from a mission where I had lived and ministered some years before who drove nearly 80 miles one snowy Christmas Day to bring us a present. And one of the best memories is of a woman testifying, "We never knew when it was Christmas until after we got saved; now we have Christmas."

Other Apache people have told me they never heard of Christmas until they went to boarding school at age 5 or 6. Even then it didn't mean anything to them. Only after they heard the gospel and accepted Christ did they realize what Christmas meant.

One man said that as a little boy in boarding school he beard what Christmas meant and about heaven and hell; but no one told him how to get to heaven. In his own words: "I heard there was a heaven, but that you can't make it if you lie or steal. I knew I had done both, so how could I make it?

"I wondered about this as I grew up. I left school, and I thought, I still don't know how 1 will make it to heaven. Should the medicine man sing for me? Or should I read the Bible?

"I got a New Testament and used to read it when I worked with the cowboys. I would read and try to understand. But I never could understand, and I kept wondering, How will I make it to heaven?"

This man's story has a merry Christmas ending, for one day a missionary came to Carrizo, his little village. The missionary preached the gospel, and the man learned how he could make it to heaven.

At first, he thought he could never stop drinking and couldn't be saved. But through the testimonies and prayers of other Indians and his wife who had become a Christian, he believed on the Lord Jesus Christ. He was saved and also completely delivered from the power of alcohol. At last he had found the way to make it to heaven!

Now Christmas has real meaning for him and his family. His

children are growing up with many happy memories of Christmas.

Happy memories, mostly of little things. But after all it's the little things in life, totaled, that make the sum of joy complete.

Remember Christmas began in a little place: "But thou, Bethlehem Ephratah, though thou be little among the thousands of Judah, yet out of thee shall he come forth..." (Micah 5:2).

So from a little place Christ came forth to give us the gifts of eternal life, peace, and fullness of joy—to make the way to heaven for us.

Have you accepted that way He made? Have you like the Apache man found out "how you can make it"? If not, let your happiest memories begin this Christmas by accepting God's gift, His Son Jesus, whom He sent into the world to save us from our sins.

ROBBED!

"Hey! Did you hear the news? Forestdale Trading Post was robbed!"

"When?"

"This evening about five. I was the first one to get there after it happened." The excited speaker was our local Apache policeman.

I thought of the elderly couple who operated the trading post. It was a ramshackle building located on a lonely stretch of reservation highway. They catered to passing tourists and were alone most of the time.

The policeman told us how two masked men armed with rifles had hidden in the dimly lighted old store. After closing time they had bound and gagged the elderly owners.

"No, they weren't harmed," he answered my unspoken question. "But," he continued, "all the turquoise and silver jewelry and the hand-woven Indian baskets were taken!"

I realized that would mean a loss of thousands of dollars. "Surely they had some insurance?"

"No," the policeman replied, "they didn't—and they sure were crying." I knew these people had been warned of the danger of robbery. In fact, they had even experienced one small theft—a few pieces of jewelry taken from a showcase by a shoplifter. The guilty party was soon caught, the jewelry returned.

After that locks had been put on the glass showcases where the beautiful turquoise and silver jewelry was displayed. Evidently they felt safe with the locks on the glass cases. "Anyway," they had said, "we have been here for many years, and nothing serious has ever happened to us." They seemed to believe if they treated people fairly and were good to everyone, they would be all right. Now they had been robbed and had no insurance, because of misplaced trust.

I felt sorry for them. But there is something worse. It is possible to be robbed of eternal possessions.

The Bible warns of a terrible thief: "Verily, verily, I say unto you, He that entereth not by the door into the sheepfold but climbeth up some other way, the same is a thief and a robber" (John 10:1). How many people realize too late that they have been robbed by this thief and have no insurance for eternity!

People put their trust in church membership, in being sincere, in being religious, in being tolerant. But these are just locks on glass cases. They are no problem for the thief; in fact, he is pleased with the false sense of security these give. Death smashes the glass case of life, and the thief takes the soul and the hope of eternal life.

Of course, some feel like death is what always happens to

someone else. How foolish! Listen to Hebrews 9:27:"It is appointed unto men once to die, but after this the judgment."

Then there are people who trust in their own righteousness, their good works. Hear what the Bible says:"But we are all as an unclean thing, and all our righteousnesses are as filthy rags" (Isaiah 64:6). Or read Ephesians 2:8-9:"For by grace are ye saved through faith; and that not of yourselves: it is the gift of God: not of works, lest any man should boast."

What then shall we trust? Is there any insurance possible against the thief? Yes, there is absolute assurance available, a door to safety. That door is Christ. Turn to John's Gospel and read His words:"I am the door: by me if any man enter in, he shall be saved" (John 10:9).

In verse 10 of the same chapter Christ contrasted the purpose of the thief and His purpose:"The thief cometh not, but for to steal, and to kill, and to destroy: I am come that they might have life, and that they might have it more abundantly."

In verse 11 Christ explained how He as the good Shepherd paid the premium once and for all on our insurance against the thief."The good shepherd giveth his life for the sheep." So with His own blood he made it impossible for us to ever be robbed of that which has eternal value.

Impossible to be robbed—if we meet the only requirement, accepting by faith what He has done. John 3:16 says it simply and beautifully:"For God so loved the world, that he gave his only begotten Son, that whosoever believed' in him should not perish, but have everlasting life."

What are you trusting? Your future on the other side of that doorway called death is at stake. Your insurance for eternity depends on your trust in Christ as Savior. Don't be robbed!

SAFE IN HIS ARMS

A ride on the Sandia Peak Aerial Tramway at Albuquerque, New Mexico, is a memorable experience. This tram has a clear and unsupported span of 7,700 feet, the longest in North America. It climbs up the west side of the rugged Sandia Mountains for a distance of 2.7 miles.

The journey is accomplished in about 10 minutes by two 60-passenger cars. It is a thrilling ride, and the view from a mile above the city is breathtaking.

The summer day a friend and I rode the tram there were only a few passengers. Among them bounced a small blond boy, with sparkling blue eyes, about 4 years old. He was so excited; he seemed to be everywhere at once.

As I watched the vivacious youngster, I wondered which of the young couples claimed him as their son.

He was the first person to board the passenger car, and he dashed from window to window. Several people smiled and spoke to him, but he disdained their efforts at friendliness.

When the car began to lift from the ground, I turned my full attention to the scene below. I forgot the little boy who didn't seem to want to belong to anyone. I was amazed to find that Tower 1 is 259 feet high, the tallest structure in New Mexico, and leans at an angle of 18 degrees, almost twice as much as the Leaning Tower of Pisa.

As the car climbed higher and higher, I watched with a strange fascination and very weak knees. The ground below seemed to fall away and the side of the mountain loomed before us. The view was spectacular!

Suddenly a loud wail echoed through the car. "Daddy, Daddy, hold me!"

Every head turned; the little boy, now very pale, was standing on one of the seats gripping the handrail. He was peering out the window, gazing in horror at the ground far below.

Quickly and without a word, a young man standing nearby leaned over and wrapped both arms around the shaking child.

The transformation was almost magical! The bright smile returned, the eyes again sparkled, and the look of fear was replaced with one of curiosity as he continued to peer out the window. He was safe in Daddy's arms!

Everyone was smiling now. It was obvious the child had no confidence in the powerful steel cables that carried our car. Neither the engineers' skill nor the tram's safety record impressed him. None of these facts spoke peace to his heart nor quieted his fears. But the strength of his daddy's arms was different. That was security!

As I watched this little drama, I thought about my own life. What was I trusting in? What was I leaning on? I felt a great peace when I realized that, like the little boy, I too had a Father's arms about me.

I remembered the words of Moses in his final address to the

people of Israel; "The eternal God is thy refuge, and underneath are the everlasting arms" (Deuteronomy 33:27).

For the little boy, the circumstances had not changed; but he had no fear now, for he was in his father's arms. In his fear the little boy had cried out to a loving father who was always nearby, a father who had never left him, even when the child had totally ignored him.

Where do you find safety? What spells security for you? Is it in the "everlasting arms" of your Heavenly Father? Those unseen arms of God reach out to undergird, to strengthen, to hold each of us. Sometimes it takes trouble to teach us how close our Father is to us and how quickly He will enfold us in His everlasting arms of love when we cry out to.

Moses reminded the people: The eternal God is thy refuge." He is your shelter, the place provided for your protection. Do you know about that shelter where you can take refuge when the sorrows, pain, and disappointments of life sweep over you?

Have you learned to lean on Him? Have you learned to let those "everlasting arms" support you in every circumstance when your own strength is inadequate?

Those loving arms once were extended in agony on the rough wooden cross. They were nailed there to provide the refuge, the mercy, the hope, the salvation you need.

Those same arms reach out to you today. Those arms are open to you, wherever you are, whatever your need. It matters not what your circumstances, your nationality, your creed, or your personality may be.

Your Heavenly Father is there close to you. Cry out to Him as the little boy on the tram cried out to his father. You will discover that the eternal God is your refuge, and underneath you there are everlasting arms.

SHALL WE LEAVE THEM ALONE?

This woman knows the joy of the Lord, I thought, as the smiling Indian woman approached me. Her countenance seemed to glow as she said, "Welcome to Fort Hall, Sister Craver. We have been praying for you."

Her name was Julia Coby, and in the months that followed I discovered that Julia's joy was just as deep and steadfast through every trial as it was on that sunny morning.

I asked her to help me with visitation. With Julia by my side doors were opened in welcome when we knocked. We were invited into lovely new homes and very humble homes. Julia would introduce me and then joyously witness about Jesus. She would tell what He had done for her, ending with an invitation to come to church. Many of the people we visited are now coming to church.

Sometimes well-meaning people ask concerning my work among the American Indian, "Why take them the gospel? Why invite them to church? Don't they worship the great spirit? They have their own religion. Why not leave them alone?"

Leave them alone? Without Christ, without hope? Julia was once alone in her Indian religion. I'll let her tell you about it:

I grew up in Owyhee on the Duck Valley Reservation in Nevada. My father and mother were strong peyote* people. In peyote worship, they talk about God our father and Jesus our brother, but they pray to the peyote. They believe the peyote will help them. They are afraid to say anything bad about peyote. It might hurt them.

But I was not afraid of peyote. For, deep in my heart, I did not believe in its power. I just felt empty and alone. I often wondered when I was growing up if there was a God.

Once I had a strange dream. I thought I was standing on a hill when I heard a trumpet blowing. I looked up and saw a beautiful light. Then I looked down and saw the people. Some were drinking; some were gambling; and some were fighting. They could not see the light, nor could they hear the trumpet. I never forgot that dream. I had no idea then what it meant.

The years passed. I grew up, got married, and had a baby girl; but I was still alone. There was no joy or peace in my heart.

Then some people came to Owyhee and held a meeting in the school gymnasium. I told my husband I was going, for I was curious about these meetings. I took my baby girl with me. As soon as I entered the gym, I could feel something special.

When the people started singing it sounded so beautiful! I felt as if they were singing just to me. The sermon seemed to be just for me. When the altar call was given I pushed my baby into someone's arms and ran to the front. I knelt there saying, "Jesus, Jesus." Christians prayed with me, and I felt a heavy burden lift from my heart. I got up feeling so clean!

Christians talked to me after the service and advised me to go to church. I didn't know anything about a full-gospel church, since there was none in Owyhee. After they left I went to the church that was there (Presbyterian); but somehow I could not feel the presence of Jesus. I finally stopped going, but I kept on praying secretly at home.

One day two couples came to Owyhee. When they came to visit me I knew they were God's people! One couple, Brother and Sister Roy Nelson, told me they would be coming as missionaries.

The Nelsons rented a house and started having services. I was one of the few persons who attended. My husband didn't seem to care that I went, but my parents, brothers, and sisters persecuted me. I tried to talk to them, but they only became angry with me.

Then my mother had a stroke and was in the hospital. When she came home she was quite depressed. Mom did not want to talk to anyone; she just seemed to give up. Dad kept taking her to peyote meetings, and I kept telling her about Jesus.

About that time a couple from Nampa, Idaho, Brother and Sister Edsel Horn, came to help the Nelsons. Brother Horn held a tent meeting which I will never forget. I finally persuaded Mom to go with me one night to the service.

At the close of the service I told her I would go forward with her for prayer, so she said, "All right." At the altar I told Brother Nelson, "My mom really needs prayer." They prayed for her, and she prayed as best she could. She could only say "yes, yes," to everything because she understood little of the English language.

The next morning I heard Mom calling excitedly, "Come here, come here." I rushed to her. She told me that a beautiful lady in a white robe with a shining face had visited her in her dream. This lady told her to read John 3:16 in the Bible.

"Quick, get your Bible and read it," Mom said. So I read it to her and explained what it meant. Mom began to cry. "So that's the way it is," she said, "so simple, right in front of us." We prayed together and Mom believed; from that day on she has loved and served Jesus. She also received her healing. In a short time her face straightened, her voice became normal, and her pain was gone!

We started praying for Dad. He was bitter and would yell, "You two going to church again!" every time we left the house. We just kept praying and inviting him to come with us. Finally because he felt so left out, he started going with us. But Dad said he could never let go of peyote.

Then one night Dad gave his heart to Jesus. He truly became a new man! He told Mom, "We don't need this peyote stuff anymore. What shall we do with it?" Mom said, "Let's ask Brother Nelson."

Pastor Nelson said, "If you really are going to serve the Lord, gather up that stuff and burn it!"

Dad replied, "I served peyote for many years; it never really helped me. But I know the Lord hears and answers my prayers; I'll burn it."

We went home and made a big fire. In went the drumstick, the pipe, everything connected with the peyote meeting! When we came to the medicine, the peyote itself, Dad looked at it and suddenly tossed it to the chickens that were scratching around in the yard. The chickens quickly ate it up. We all laughed at the chickens eating what used to be our god.

Dad is old now, but he is still strong and active. He never returned to the old way. He says: "If I was not serving Jesus I probably would have been dead long ago!"

Oh, I must tell you another wonderful thing the Lord did for my mother. I always read the Bible to her because she didn't understand much English. She could not read or write English. When my husband and I moved to Nampa, Mom was so sad! Now who will read the Bible to us? she wondered. Sister Nelson encouraged her to pray and ask the Lord to give her understanding.

One day in Nampa I got a letter from Mom and could hardly believe it. She wrote, "The Lord help me to read Bible, to write letter." Today Mom reads the Bible and explains it clearly in her own language to older people. She tells older Christians, "Pray and believe; the Lord will teach you to read the Bible!"

At a camp meeting in Nampa my husband gave his heart to the Lord, and later his grandmother was saved. Since then we have seen others in our family come to the Lord. The sister who persecuted me most is now the Sunday school superintendent at the Assemblies of God church in McDermitt, Nevada! God has been so good to us! He has answered our prayers and helped us through these years.

The Holy Spirit did not leave Julia alone. Surely He gave her that dream so long ago. I think of the dream. No one heard the trumpet; no one saw the light. Today thousands of Indian people still think Jesus is only the white man's God. Shall we leave them alone?

Thousands of Indians have never heard that Christ is the Light. Shall we leave them alone? There are 22 districts in 28 states in our Movement that have an Indian population, but NO Indian work. Shall we leave them alone?

Someday the trumpet that Julia heard in her dream will sound forth with a mighty blast. If we have failed to reach the Indian people of our nation, they will then, indeed, be left alone.

*Editor's Note: Peyote has two definitions: 1. Any of several cacti of the southwestern U.S. And northern Mexico, especially, mescal; 2. A stimulant drug derived from mescal buttons and used in religious ceremonials by some Indian peoples.

THAT BEAUTIFUL SONG

It was dark now, and the many sounds of night in an Apache Indian village filled the ears of the waiting man. Somewhere in the distance dogs barked and children laughed. He could hear voices, some loud and angry, others as soft as the whispering breeze. The man sat alone in the car in the darkness, waiting, listening.

Now he could hear voices coming from within the nearby building. Many voices joined together blending into song, then prayer. Sometimes he could distinguish words, phrases, but mostly it sounded only noisy. An irreverent noise at that, he thought.

"I know how people should act in church," he said to himself. "They should be quiet, not making all that noise, not clapping their hands and not shouting.

Sitting there alone in the darkness he pondered his reason for even being there—outside the East Fork Community Church.

He remembered when he was a young Apache boy, many years ago, starting to boarding school. He had been baptized by the Protestant missionary and told he belonged to that particular church. He had stayed in that church all through school. When he got out of school, he even acted as an interpreter for the missionary.

Then becoming dissatisfied he had gone into Catholicism, and for years he had considered himself a good Catholic. But because of something that had happened in his life, he had been told he could no longer go to confession or take Communion. Now what was he to do?

Then one day his wife told him, "I hear they are going to have a revival at the East Fork Community Church; let's go down there."

Very reluctantly he agreed to take her to "that church." But he would not go inside; he would sit in the car and wait for her.

So night after night he sat alone in the darkness and listened, in spite of himself, to the sounds of the service going on inside. That night, sitting there deep in thought, he suddenly realized they were singing a beautiful song.

He rolled the window down and leaned far out of the car trying to catch all of the words. Never had he heard a song like that! He thought about it the rest of the evening. The next day it seemed to ring over and over in his mind.

That evening he said to his wife, "Let's go down to that church again." This time he decided he would stand by the car so he could hear better in case they sang that beautiful song. After a few more nights he thought he would stand just outside the door where he could hear even better.

Then one night he decided to go inside. I'll sit as close to the door as possible, he thought, so I can get out in a hurry if anything happens.

The people did sing the beautiful song again. He could hear and understand every word. Its message touched his heart in a strange way.

He went forward and accepted Christ as his own Savior. It was as if a great light shined into his heart and the way opened before him, clear and bright. He no longer sat alone in the darkness!

Not long afterward while in prayer he had a vision. He saw many Apache people wandering here and there. He knew they were lost. Then in his vision he saw a group of Apache women sitting on the ground, as Apache women sometimes do. As he approached, he could hear them singing. When he got nearer, he realized they were singing that beautiful song. He could hear the words:

Amazing grace! 'how sweet the sound,
That saved a wretch like me!
I once was lost, but now am found, Was blind but now I see.

With great joy in his heart he realized he was now one of those "noisy Christians." Now he too could sing that beautiful song! He could and would share its message with his people.

This happened more than 10 years ago. Today Nelson Lupe, the man whose heart was touched by a beautiful song, is pastor of a full-gospel church.

Brother Lupe, for many years prior to and after his conversion, has held places of leadership and responsibility on the reservation. He is highly esteemed by all who know him.

One of Brother Lupe's sons, Eddie, is a second-year student at the American Indian Bible Institute, Phoenix, Ariz. Eddie's inspiring testimony appeared in the summer 1976 edition of Slant magazine in the article, "A Visit to Apache Land."

THE DAY I PRAYED
FOR A VACUUM CLEANER

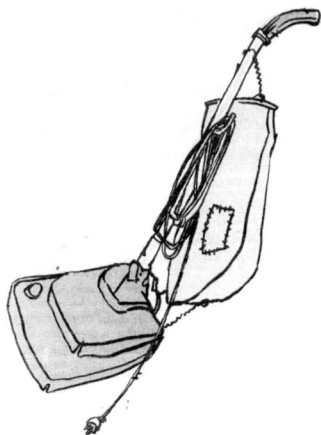

I shall never forget the day I prayed for a vacuum cleaner, an old vacuum cleaner.

I don't mean prayed for in the sense that I had an old cleaner that needed a divine touch to make it swallow up the dust again. No, I mean I needed a vacuum cleaner. I was fighting a losing battle against the dust that the relentless wind drove into my house.

It gets dusty here in Arizona when it has not rained in months. The swirling winds (dust devils, appropriately named) will sweep across the floor of Carrezo Canyon where we live. Everything loose will go with the wind in a cloud of red dust rising skyward—seeming always to descend on or near our house. Dust came seeping in around the windows, under the doors, and through cracks we never knew existed.

I was battling this with broom and mop one very windy day when I just stopped, bowed my head, and prayed. I remember the words: "O Lord, You know I need a vacuum cleaner, and surely someone has an old cleaner they will give me."

It was a short but fervent prayer. Then I went back to my war with the dust.

A week or so later, some friends stopped to see me. "Could you by chance use an old vacuum cleaner?" they asked.

"Oh, yes," I hastily replied—adding, "Praise the Lord."

So it wasn't long until I was trying to clean the house with my "old vacuum cleaner." It had many foibles. For one thing, the on and off switch didn't always work. You had to plug and unplug it to start and stop.

That wasn't so bad, but usually fire would fly out of it when I plugged it in or unplugged it. And sometimes black smoke would come boiling forth from somewhere within the thing, and I would have to make a mad dash to the outlet to unplug it.

Worst of all, it was very particular about the type of dirt it would pick up. It spurned most of the dust as something beneath its notice.

On another windy day when I was struggling with my "old vacuum cleaner," trying valiantly to clean up the dust, I once again cried out to the Lord: "O Lord, how can I ever keep this house clean with this old vacuum cleaner?"

I really wasn't expecting an answer—but deep within my heart I seemed to hear these words: "Isn't this what you asked for, an old vacuum cleaner? I could have given you a new one just as easily, but you asked for an old vacuum cleaner."

I was stunned—abashed, as I realized what I had done. I bowed my head and asked the Lord to forgive me for asking for a crumb when I could have had a whole loaf.

Since that day I have tried never to limit God.

I am sure there are many times when our Heavenly Father desires to do "exceeding abundantly above all that we ask or think, according to the power that worketh in us" (Ephesians 3:20). Most of us live below our privileges—not just in the material realm, but also in the spiritual. How many burdens we carry! Oh, what needless pain we bear! How much joy leaks out of our hearts! How many thoughts about yesterday or tomorrow torment us because we fail to cast our burdens upon the Lord.

We have not, because we ask not, the Word says. "Ask, and ye shall receive, that your joy may be full" (John 16:24).

We forget that even the tiniest bird is entered on our Father's inventory sheet. "Ye are of more value than many sparrows" (Matthew 10:31).

"Trust Me," the Lord is saying. "I will supply all your needs. I delight to do so. I will not reprimand you for asking too much, for I love to give with a liberal measure."

Remember: though He is able to supply an old vacuum cleaner, He would much rather give you a new one. Just ask!

P.S. Not long after this, some other friends brought me a fine vacuum cleaner—not a new one, but one that worked very well. They said I could use it until I was able to get another. Later the WMCs of the Potomac District (my home district) gave me an offering to buy a washer, dryer, floor scrubber and polisher—and a new vacuum sweeper!

How generous the Lord is!

THE GIFT OF GOD

It was an exciting night in the Apache Assembly of God, at Carrizo, Arizona. It was the night of the Christmas program—and an especially happy night for me. After years of putting together Christmas programs, years of worrying about missing Wise Men, gum-chewing angels, forgotten lines, and lost halos, I had finally been able to turn the whole thing over to a young Apache couple.

Delbert Childs and his wife Rosie, who had helped me with the program the past year, felt that they could do it alone this year; and I was glad to turn it over to them.

For several weeks prior to Christmas their pickup truck would pull into the churchyard full of laughing, singing young people and smaller children. They would troop into the church for practice. I did not attend, but Rosie kept me informed of their progress.

One Saturday morning she came to the house for coat hangers. "I am going to have really nice halos for the angel choir," she explained.

While I hunted for extra hangers, she went on to say: "I told Delbert and my brother they couldn't go deer hunting until we made the halos!"

I found some hangers for her, and later that afternoon she returned to show us a glittering array of beautiful halos.

Rosie seemed troubled about only one thing. They had asked

another young couple (the man had just started coming to church) to be Mary and Joseph. Though they had consented, seeming pleased to be asked, they had not been able to come to practice.

"Oh well," Rosie said, "they only have to come in and sit; they don't say anything, and surely they'll come for dress rehearsal."

But Mary and Joseph did not make it to dress rehearsal. The young man, a policeman, had to work that night. His wife, a teacher's aide, was required to attend a school function. But they still wanted to be in the program, Rosie told me. "It is up to you," I answered.

At last it was the night of the program. The church was filled with smiling people. You could see excitement sparkling in the eyes of the children. The couple who were to be Mary and Joseph arrived and hurried off to the Sunday school room to don their costumes. Only a few minutes longer and the program would start!

Then Rosie, a worried look on her face, hurried toward me. When she got to where I was greeting people, she whispered, "Sister Jo Ann, what will we do? That robe won't fit Mary; it's too small! And you know what? I forgot to bring a doll to put in the cradle to be Baby Jesus. Oh, Sister Jo Ann, what will we do?"

I comforted her saying, "Don't worry; we'll think of something." But I was far from confident. I doubted if there was another blue robe, or a robe of any suitable kind for that matter, in the whole village. Why hadn't I remembered that always before one of the slender young girls had taken the part of Mary?

We went into the Sunday school room where Apache angels of all sizes, adorned with glittering halos, stood silently, their black eyes wide and questioning.

Mary, looking embarrassed, was struggling unsuccessfully to make the robe meet. "It just won't go around me," she said, almost in tears.

Her husband, our Joseph, was struggling to keep back the laughter at the sight of his wife trying so hard to fit into the obviously too small robe. Suddenly the humor of it all overcame me, and I started to laugh. Oh boy, I thought, this is the one program I didn't have to worry about!

My laughter broke the tension. Soon the small room was filled with quiet laughter as the others joined in. Suddenly I took another look at our Mary; she had given up on the robe and tossed it onto a chair.

She was wearing a beautiful, dark blue satin Apache-style dress called a camp dress —a long skirt with a full over blouse, both trimmed with white rick-rack. "Hey," I said, "you look beautiful. Just be yourself, an Apache woman acting out the part of Mary. You don't need a robe!"

"Just go out there in my dress?" she asked doubtfully.

"Sure. I think that will look just fine," I answered.

"But what about a baby doll for the manger?" asked Rosie.

"Oh, let Crystal be the baby," someone suggested. Crystal was a tiny baby, and I knew her mother had brought her. They were already out in the congregation.

"That's a good idea," I said, and so someone dashed out to get the baby.

Now at last the program had begun. A tiny Apache girl gave a welcome. This was followed by prayer and congregational singing and then recitations. I stood in the back watching it all with a great sense of joy.

Finally it was time for the main part of the program—the result of all the work, all the happy rehearsals. The lights, except for those on the platform, were turned off. Delbert, the narrator who usually spoke so softly you had to strain your ears to hear him, was reading in a loud, clear voice.

The scenes unfolded smoothly—the angels, the shepherds, the songs. Then it was time for Mary and Joseph and the baby to come on. When the curtains opened on that scene, our Mary looked radiant in her blue satin camp dress; baby Crystal lay quietly in the makeshift manger. All the lights were out now except the light from a large beautiful star that swayed over them.

I remembered how Delbert, an artistic young man, had made that star from cardboard and glitter. He had suspended it by an unseen wire and had improvised a light to shine through it.

Delbert continued to read: "The silence of the night was broken by a baby's cry." As if she knew that was her cue, little Crystal started to cry!

Mary and Joseph leaned together toward the manger; then Joseph lifted the baby and handed it to Mary. There was a hush in the church. Even the narrator paused as Mary quieted the baby.

I stood in the back of the darkened church and looked through a mist of .tears at the scene before me. This is Christmas, I thought; this is really Christmas.

I was aware of the presence of Christ, who comes to us just as we are. Our Mary, in her Apache dress rather than a robe, spoke to me of the fact that God will accept us as we are. He will blend us into His great program that stretches across eternity.

I looked at the homemade star, transformed into a thing of delicate beauty by the light that shone through it. How like what Christ, the Light of the world, does for us! He will shine through us and touch our ordinary lives with glory.

"Unto you a Savior is born," the narrator boldly declared. The angels began to sing, and the darkened church was filled with the beautiful words of hope: "Joy to the world; the Lord is come!"

Yes, truly the Lord is come, I thought, as in the dim light I picked out people in the congregation, both men and women, whose lives had been transformed by Christ. People whose lives were once hopeless, whose hearts were once crushed by the heavy load of sin—to them the Lord had come, indeed!

Then I looked at others there in the dim shadows who were still struggling in sin and despair. I thought of the multitudes just like them across the world who would try to celebrate Christmas without a heart knowledge of Christ. The words Jesus spoke to that lonely, empty-hearted Samaritan woman came to my mind: "If thou knewest the gift of God..." (John 4:10).

The "Gift of God," the Christ who will accept you just as you are, no costume needed, no pretense. Oh, the "Gift of God," Christ the Light who will transform your life and let His light shine through you, giving you hope and peace.

The program ended, and the lights came on. Our Christmas gifts for the people were distributed, and we received many gifts from our people. But the best gift of all was the "Gift of God." We could say with thankful hearts, "Thank God for his Son, his gift too wonderful for words" (2 Corinthians 9:15, Living Bible paraphrased).

The foregoing story is reprinted from Assemblies of God Home Missions, the new magazine published bimonthly by the Division of Home Missions. It is mailed free to interested friends on request.

THE GOD WHO LOVES US

Starlene, Starlene, get up!

Her mother's sharp voice broke into her sleep. Starlene sat up, took a deep breath. And sniffed the strong smell of coffee boiling on the fire outside the wickiup.

"Hurry," Mother called loudly, the sun is already in the sky."

Throwing aside the blanket, Starlene jumped up and stood shivering by the remains of the small fire in the center of the wickiup. The dirt floor felt warm to her bare feet. She was already dressed because she had slept in her clothes.

With a sigh Starlene stepped outside into the crisp fall morning. Without saying a word she started to run toward the creek that flowed along the base of the red hills, near the clearing where their camp was built.

Reaching the creek, Starlene stopped only a moment before plunging into the clear, cold water. She went completely under, then swam to the top, gasping for breath. Her body felt numb as she quickly climbed up the creek bank and dashed across the frosty ground. It was so cold that icicles formed in her long black hair; they jingled like bells as she raced toward the wickiup and the fire.

Starlene, a little Apache Indian girl who lived on the Fort Apache Reservation in Arizona. had been taught that it made a girl strong and healthy to run to the creek and jump in every morning—even when jumping in meant breaking the ice!

Starlene returned to the camp of her mother's family. They lived in wickiups, made by tying poles together at the top and thatching them with heavy grass. The Carrizo Creek was their water source.

Running barefoot across the hard ground, trying to avoid the plants with stickers, Starlene thought how much she hated doing this on cold mornings. When she went away to boarding school, at least she wouldn't be here in the winter to run to the creek.

Thinking about going to school scared Starlene. She should have gone this year. Smiling to herself, she recalled how she had hidden from the Indian policeman who came looking for the children to take to the boarding school in Whiteriver.

When Starlene got back to the wickiup, her mother said, "Put on your dry clothes; eat your tortilla, and drink your coffee. Hurry, we have much work to do before the ceremony."

Nervousness was in her mother's voice. Starlene knew her mother spoke sharply because she was so worried. Baby Brother was sick he cried and cried. No matter what Mother did, he seemed only to grow worse.

"Your father left before daylight to get the medicine man," Mother said. "We must have the camp clean and ready when he returns.'

Starlene nodded. She felt afraid as she listened to the crying baby. Mother held him in his cradle board, rocking it gently.

By the time Father and the medicine man arrived, Starlene and the rest of the women in the camp had cleaned and swept the ground around the wickiups. They were ready. Starlene stood at the edge of the silent group of people who had gathered for the ceremony.

The aged medicine man first built a small fire, then he carefully spread out the new blanket which Mother provided. On the blanket he prepared all the things he needed.

Starlene knew the reason for working on the blanket. Everything the medicine man used must be kept together, in one place. When the ceremony was over, all of it would be taken out of the camp and hidden where no one could find it. It would be dangerous to bother the things the medicine man had used.

The old medicine man took a small piece of the center stalk of a bear grass plant and carefully cleaned it, scraping off the bark. As he worked, he sang the sacred songs that had to do with this ceremony.

When the stalk was cleaned, he slowly carved it into the shape of a snake. Using some ashes from the fire, he made stripes on the sides of the carved snake; on the flattened end that was the head he made eyes.

When it was finished, the medicine man put the end with the head into the fire. As soon as it began to burn, he pulled it out and held it as he watched the flames die out.

Starlene and the others watched in fearful silence. The only sound was the crackling fire and the old medicine man's voice, which grew more powerful as it rose and fell with the chanting.

While the charred head of the carved snake was still very hot, the medicine man bit it off. Starlene gasped as he slowly chewed it, and then blew it on Baby Brother. He kept chanting the prayers for a long time.

That night Baby Brother did not cry. He lay still in his cradle board, struggling for every breath. Rolled in her blanket by the fire, Starlene listened with a sad heart to her mother's soft voice trying to comfort the baby.

Just as morning came creeping over the red hills, Starlene was jolted awake by a loud wailing cry. It was her mother's voice. Jumping to her feet, she heard her father speaking words of comfort to her mother, but he too was crying. Starlene looked at him in wonder; she had never seen him cry. Starlene didn't ask questions—she knew. Baby Brother was dead.

Later that day friends and relatives gathered to have a wake. They sat quietly by the fires that were burning near the wickiups. The women helped cook over the open fires and everyone ate together. They ate again at midnight.

When morning came, they went to the burial place on the slope of one of the red hills. Almost in sight of the wickiup where Baby Brother spent his short life. Some of the men had dug a rough hole in the red earth and lined it with branches from the cedar trees that grew on the hillside.

The little board box that held Baby Brother was dropped into the empty hole. Starlene shuddered at the hollow, thudding sound of the box hitting the bottom of the grave.

Her face was wet with tears as she helped the women put Baby Brother's clothes, his blankets, and a few toys into the grave. They also put in milk and other kinds of food. Last of all they put in a new Pendleton blanket. Father made the long trip yesterday on his horse. down the canyon to the trading post to buy the blanket to put in the grave.

Finally the men cut more cedar branches and placed them on top of the blanket. Then they took turns shoveling the red dirt back into the hole. When it was piled in a high mound, someone brought a flat rock that had Baby Brother's name, birth date, and the date of his death chiseled on its smooth surface.

As everyone watched, the rock was firmly pushed into the side of the mound of red dirt. Then the medicine man took a small bucket of ashes. Chanting softly he circled the grave with scattering ashes. One of the women came to Mother and took the empty cradle board out of her arms and hung it in the branches of a cedar tree growing near the grave.

It was over. Everyone started back to the camp; Starlene walked close to her mother. Her father walked with the other men.

Her mother was still crying; she spoke softly between her sobs. "Why did he die? Why? We paid the medicine man well. We did everything we knew to do. Why isn't there a God who loves people? Why? Why? Why?"

Sadly, Starlene turned and looked back at the mound of red dirt. The cradle board was swinging gently in the wind that moved through the branches of the cedar trees. It sounded to Starlene like the wind was crying too. It seemed to echo her mother's words: Why? Why? Why?

Starlene and her family moved right away after burying Baby Brother. No one would ever live in those wickiups again, death had taken someone in that camp. Who knew what spirits would come there now? They made a new camp farther up the canyon, but still close to the sparkling waters of Carrizo Creek.

The days rushed by. It was fall again. Mother said, "This year you must go to Whiteriver to the boarding school, Starlene."

Somehow with Baby Brother gone, Starlene didn't mind leaving. So one bright day when the leaves on the cottonwood trees were starting to glisten like gold, she got in the truck with the other children to go to Whiteriver.

Starlene had her clothes tied in a bundle in her blanket. Her new shoes hurt her feet, but she was off to school!

School was hard and strange—sitting for hours on hard chairs, trying to understand what the white people who ran the school wanted her to do. She didn't know much of their language. Eating, oh, eating was the worst of all! The food was so different, and forks and spoons were so hard to use.

For many days Starlene was homesick. She missed her parents, she missed being free to run and play. She even missed running to the creek every morning.

Little by little Starlene adjusted to the school. Becky, the girl whose bed was closest to hers in the dorm, helped her understand things. Becky had been to school for 2 years now, so she knew more about the ways of white people.

Becky was a different type of girl too. She was kind, no matter what happened, and always had a smile for everyone. After a while, Starlene began to wonder about Becky.

Finally one day as they worked together making their beds, Starlene asked, "Becky, why are you so nice to everyone?"

Becky just smiled.

Starlene continued, "Even when someone teases you, or when the teacher scolds you and it isn't your fault, you don't cry like I do. You don't get mad and fight either. Why, Becky?"

Becky smiled again. If you really want to know I'll take you to find out."

"Take me to find out?" Starlene was puzzled. "Why don't you

just tell me?"

"No. Starlene, I'll take you. Then you must find out for yourself. If you want to go, I'll ask permission to take you to the Bible story class."

"The Bible story class!" Starlene exclaimed. "Is that where some of the kids go every Thursday?" Then slowly she asked, "Is it church?"

Starlene had learned about church and she didn't like it. Every Sunday they were marched to the church, sat in hard pews with poor light, and sang strange songs. They were told to be good, don't steal, don't lie, don't fight. But everyone did those things. Well, almost everyone, Starlene thought as she looked at Becky.

Becky broke into her thoughts. "No," she said, "it isn't church. But if you go find out, then maybe you'll like church better."

"OK, I'll go," Starlene agreed.

On Thursday Becky received permission to take Starlene to the room where the Bible story class was held. About a dozen children were there. Starlene noticed a smiling white woman who welcomed each child. Her soft voice made Starlene feel a pain of longing for her mother.

The white woman said "Let's sing." This was a different kind of singing than they did in church, but it didn't make any more sense to Starlene. Yet she liked the way it sounded, so when the white woman and the other children started to clap their hands to the song, Starlene shyly joined in.

The white woman said, "I am Marilyn, and I am glad you have come to Bible story class. Let's all say our class Scripture verse together."

Starlene listened in amazement to the words the children were saying: "For God so loved the world that he gave his one and only

Son, that whoever believes in him shall not per ish but have eternal life" (John 3:16, NIV).

Starlene's mind raced back to the day they buried her baby brother. She could almost hear her mother asking, "Why isn't there a God who loves people? Why? Why? Why?"

Starlene was so caught up in her memories and the amazing words telling about a God who loves people, she was unaware of what else was said.

When it was over, she could hardly wait until they were out of the room to start asking questions. "Becky, Becky, where is the God who loves the world? Why did He give His Son? What kind of ceremony do we have to go through to believe in Him?"

"You'll have to come back next week and listen to everything Marilyn says," Becky replied. "She explains it best. You weren't listening tonight—it was probably too much for you to take in at once."

It was a long week, but finally Thursday came. Starlene felt excited as she and Becky joined the other children in the Bible story class. This time she listened to every word.

They sang a happy song, then it was time to say the Bible verse, "For God so loved. . ." Again Starlene was almost overcome with wonder. There was a God who loved people!

Then Marilyn held up some large colored pictures and began to tell them about each one. It was about people who lived long ago. They did not obey God and were punished by being bitten by snakes.

Starlene shuddered.

One picture showed a man with a snake on a pole. Marilyn said, "This man's name is Moses. God told Moses to tell the people to look at the snake lifted up on the pole and they would live. If they refused to look, they would die."

Starlene thought about the medicine man and the snake he had carved the day of the ceremony. "That snake didn't help my baby brother," she thought with anger.

Marilyn showed them another picture, one that scared Starlene. It was a picture of a man with a kind, sad face. He was nailed to a wooden cross. There was blood on His hands and feet.

"This is Jesus, God's Son—the Son He gave for us because He loves us," Marilyn said. "Jesus never lied, stole, or disobeyed. But everyone of us have done those things and many other things that displease God. We have sinned. We were all born into the world as sinners and we should die for our sins. Jesus was willing to die in our place."

Marilyn paused and looked around. Then she continued, "Just as the man named Moses lifted up that snake on a pole and the people who believed and obeyed were saved from death, Jesus was lifted up on the cross. He died for us! If we believe and obey, we too will be saved. We won't be punished forever after we die, but we shall go on living with God.

"Because," Marilyn said, as she showed a beautiful picture of Jesus standing by a big rock near a cave, "Jesus died on that cross. He was buried in this cave, but after 3 days He walked out of the cave alive!"

"Alive?!" Starlene exclaimed aloud.

The other children turned to look at Starlene.

"That's all right," Marilyn said. She smiled. "Yes indeed. Jesus is alive! Many people saw Him. They even saw Him go up in a cloud to heaven.

"Jesus said He will come to each of us if we will be sorry for our sin, ask Him to forgive us, and invite Him to live within us.

Think of it." Marilyn said as she finished, "Jesus will come and live in you and give you peace and joy. You can know Him, for He is the God who loves you."

As soon as the class was over Starlene hurried to Marilyn. "I want to know Him," she said with tears running down her cheeks. "Please, I want to know the God who loves people."

Marilyn put her arms around Starlene and, motioning for Becky to join them, they prayed together. Starlene asked Jesus to come into her life and to forgive her sin and change her life.

When she had finished praying, Starlene turned to Becky with a smile. "Now I know why you said you would take me to find out. I had to pray for myself, didn't I?"

Becky's smile was bigger than ever. She nodded her head.

"Oh, Becky," Starlene said, "I can hardly wait until school is over so I can go home and tell my mother there is a God who loves people, and I know Him. I really know Him!"

THE OLD WEAVER REMEMBERS

The old woman sits quietly in the sun, her wrinkled brown face a silent testimony to the struggles and joys of her long years. Her gnarled hands move slowly, yet skillfully, as she weaves an Apache water jug, called a tus.

Perhaps she is remembering when a tus was a necessity. Now it is something that is bought by the tourist or collector of Indian artifacts. Even the art of weaving the watertight tus and the other beautiful baskets is dying. So few remember, so few want to learn.

Does she think of the baskets she has woven in the days when her eyes were keen and her teeth strong? Strong teeth were needed to split the mulberry branches to get out the soft, white inner part used for weaving. She had made many beautiful baskets with strange, lovely designs woven into them. But that was long ago when she could work hard; now she makes only the simpler tus.

This old woman sitting in the sun would tell us that much work goes into weaving a basket—from gathering the right materials and preparing them to the final weaving process. Making the design to be woven into the basket and trimming the finished basket with buckskin fringes and cone-shaped bells requires skill. Who would know, these days, even how to tan the buckskin?

Much work, much work, the old woman muses, to take the worthless mulberry branches and rough devil's claw plant, used for the black design, and turn them into a lovely useful basket.

It reminds the old one of the story the missionary told of Jesus who came into this world seeking the worthless lives of men and women. Jesus paid for their worthlessness and shame with His own blood. They killed Him in a terrible way on a cross. The missionary said it happened a long time ago.

He died, but He couldn't stay dead, for He was God's own Son! After 3 days He came back to life again. Then He went to heaven and sent another One, called the Holy Spirit, to be with us on earth.

Now the Holy Spirit seeks men and women just as the basket weaver seeks her materials. Men and women. who seem as worthless as the mulberry branches that the weaver gathers! Yet He seeks for them and He changes them. He tears the sin out of their lives as the weaver tears away the useless part of the mulberry branch. Then the Holy Spirit takes the life and begins to weave it into the shape and image of Jesus.

Ah yes, this is true, the old woman knows, for she remembers when He first began to seek after her. Many years she had wondered if there could be a God who loved people, who was kind. For she had known much sorrow, much hurt.

Then one day she heard of Him, the God who loved. His name was Jesus. He loved her!

When she began to pray to Him, He came into her life. His Holy Spirit came to her and began to weave His love and changing power into her life—just as the basket weaver changes the shape of the mulberry branches, making them into something new, beautiful, and useful. Even so He had changed her life, making it new, giving her peace and purpose for living.

Oh, there had been sorrows in this new life—the death of loved ones, disappointments, the things that come to those who live long. But He took even these and wove them together, making them blend into her days, giving her peace and comfort.

Just as the black devil's claw makes the design in the basket, the old woman thought, so our problems and troubles given into the hand of Jesus, the great Weaver, make our lives more beautiful.

It takes a long time to weave a big, beautiful basket; the weaver must keep on working until the job is done. The Holy Spirit never stops working in our lives, she murmurs to herself, until the job is done. Then He takes His finished work, the life He has sought, changed, and woven into His image, to His home in the sky.

Someday soon, the missionary said, Jesus himself would come and stand in the clouds and call all His people up to Him with a loud shout. On that day there would be no need to weave any more baskets; but now she must hurry and finish this one.

The sun is very warm; the old woman nods; her eyes close. She remembers.

THE PARABLE OF THE PEACH TREES

Planting them was the most pressing work.

What should we do about the peach trees? My friend's brother had ordered them, and they were scheduled for delivery in a few days—but in the meantime he had suffered a heart attack, so he would be unable to plant them.

Once we knew he would be all right, those 650 peach trees became the most pressing question. The holes for them had already been dug, but who would plant them?

Finally family and friends decided to go ahead and do the planting. That's why that warm February day found me out in a field that was once desert, in California's Imperial Valley. I was holding one end of a chalk line, helping mark the rows to make sure the trees would be planted straight.

Kneeling on that rough, bone-dry ground to hold the chalk line taut, I was totally engrossed with the activity around me until suddenly the words of the first Psalm began tumbling over and over in my mind.

"He shall be like a tree planted by the rivers of water." "Like a tree planted." Planted?

I almost dropped the chalk line. I had read that Psalm countless times, but never before did the meaning of the word planted reach me. I had always read it with the thought of a tree growing by the water.

Looking at the work going on around me, I realized there was a vast difference between a tree growing just anywhere and a tree planted, watered, and cultivated for a purpose. The purpose the Psalmist spoke of was the same as our purpose in planting these trees: to bear fruit!

What a great analogy, I thought. In today's vernacular the Psalmist was "right on."

I scanned the harsh terrain and glanced up at the sun, hot and brilliant even in February. What would it be like in August! This was surely not an inviting nor likely place to be planting fruit trees. And yet, with the fertilizer that even now the men were putting into each deep hole, and with adequate water (some from tank trucks now, more from an irrigation system later) these spindly, bare-root peach trees would grow and produce beautiful fruit.

Even so the Christian, the "blessed" man of Psalm 1, is planted. He grows in a desert—the harsh, uninviting spiritual desert of this world's system, where glaring evil casts its blinding light. Christians thrive in very unlikely places, like those Paul spoke of in Philippians 4:22 who were growing in "Caesar's household."

From Rome A. D. 60 to Anywhere A.D. 1984, Christians do not "just happen" to be where they are. If they are in an uninviting place, it is not by accident. They are "planted." God put them there to grow in that office, that factory, or that school. That place may seem as dark and ungodly as "Caesar's household," but they are like a tree planted, growing there for a purpose—to bear fruit!

Hear the words of Jesus: "You did not choose me, but I chose you to go and bear fruit—fruit that will last" (John 15:16, NIV).

To learn more about the comparison of fruit to the Christian life, read Romans 7:4; Philippians 1:11; and Colossians 1:10.

But remember, the little peach trees we were planting would soon have withered and died, never bearing fruit, had they not been properly planted and rooted firmly in the deep holes. They also had to be fed—enriched with fertilizer—and above all, given plenty of water.

Likewise the Word of God promises that our spiritual leaves

will never wither, nor will we fail to grow and bear fruit, if we are properly planted—even in the barren desert of this world.

We will flourish and bear fruit if, after accepting Christ Jesus as Lord, we "continue to live in him, rooted and built up in him, strengthened in the faith as you were taught, and overflowing with thankfulness" (Colossians 2:6-7, NIV).

Notice also Ephesians 3:17 which urges us to be "rooted and established in love." The nutrients vital to our fruit-bearing are faith in Christ, love, and obedience. We are sustained daily by the living water, Christ himself, through the power of the Holy Spirit. We are not "of the world"—our life comes from another source—but we are "in the world" to grow and to bear fruit.

How does this happen? It comes about as we study the Bible, develop a regular prayer time, and become part of a church family. The Psalmist called this being "planted in the house of the Lord" (Psalm 92:13, NIV). The next verse gives this wonderful promise: "They will still bear fruit in old age, they will stay fresh and green."

There was one other important thing we had to remember when we planted those little peach trees. Before they were shipped, each one of the little trees had been grafted onto the root it was growing from. It was critical to their survival that they be planted with the graft toward the west, so they could withstand the prevailing wind.

We must never forget that we Christian believers have also been grafted. We are grafted into that holy root, into the family of God! Paul explains this grafting in Romans 11:17-23.

You may be sure that against your life the prevailing wind will blow—the merciless wind of temptation. Sometimes it will blow as a gentle breeze, lulling your soul to careless, prayerless, fruitless living. Sometimes it will blow with gale force—you will be buffeted with sorrow, with pain, and with questions that seemingly have no answers.

Yes, the prevailing wind will beat against you, so it is critical to your survival that you, like the little peach trees, be facing in the right direction. The Bible puts it this way: "Let us fix our eyes on Jesus, the author and perfecter of our faith, who for the joy set before him endured the cross, scorning its shame, and sat down at the right hand of the throne of God. Consider him who endured such opposition from sinful men, so that you will not grow weary and lose heart" (Hebrews 12:2-3, NIV).

At last we had planted every one of those 650 peach trees! Of course, they would require continued care, cultivation, and pruning. Planting of itself is not enough. The analogy holds true in the spiritual life.

Remember what Jesus said: "My Father is the gardener. He cuts off every branch in me that bears no fruit, while every branch that does bear fruit He trims clean so that it will be even more fruitful" (John 15:1-2, NIV).

More fruitful! My friends are expecting an abundance of beautiful, delicious fruit. They expect a harvest that will be a blessing to them and to many other people.

Similarly the Lord expects us to become fruitful Christians. He looks for much fruit—an abundant harvest, that will be a blessing to other people. The fruit of Christ-likeness in our lives will cause others to desire to be "planted in the house of the Lord" and to grow for this same purpose, to bear fruit for Christ in the uninviting desert of this world.

The fruit that will grow on my friend's peach trees will be beautiful and delicious, I am sure; but it will also be perishable. Contrariwise the fruit of the Christian life, called the fruit of the Spirit, will never perish. That fruit of "love, joy, peace, patience, kindness, goodness, faithfulness, gentleness, and self-control" (Galatians 5:22-23, NIV) will endure forever. It will abide and bless for time and eternity.

THE PAUSE THAT REALLY REFRESHES

That summer morning I was sitting in my car by a ramshackle building that blended into the forest clearing as if it had grown there, board by weathered board.

A faded sign read, "Reservation Trading Post, Indian Crafts, etc." I was waiting for an Indian friend I had brought here to sell some beadwork.

The beauty of the place seemed to flow over me. I became aware of the tall green pines, their needles shimmering in the sunlight against the blue sky. I really saw the glistening cotton-woods, the golden glory of tiny yellow wild flowers carpeting the sides of the highway.

I breathed a prayer of thankfulness for the joy of being alive, able to see, to appreciate.

Words from that old hymn sang through my mind:

This is my Father's world, and to my list'ning ears,
All nature sings, and 'round me rings the music of the spheres.
This is my Father's world, I rest me in the thought
Of rocks and trees, of skies and seas—
His hand the wonders wrought.
—MALTIE BABCOCK

As I sat there bubbling over with praise and joy, I noticed the cars and trucks roaring by on the highway. How many of the people rushing past were unaware of this tranquil scene? How often we are in such a hurry to get there we miss what is here.

Many people go through life treating today like a bitter medicine that must be endured to reach that mystical tomorrow. Where are you going? Are you in such a rush to get there—to tomorrow with its anticipated joy—that you have missed today?

Today is all you have, and much Of it may already be gone. Over and over we read words in both Old and New Testament that speak in present tense of today. This day is the day to hear His voice, the day of salvation, etc. In short, today is the day to really begin living.

In Psalm 118:24 we read: "This is the day which the Lord hath made; we will rejoice and be glad in it."

Or we read Psalm 19:1-3: "The heavens declare the glory of God; and the firmament showeth his handiwork. Day unto day uttereth speech, and night unto night showeth knowledge. There is no speech nor language, where their voice is not heard." But their voice is heard only by those who pause to listen with their hearts as well as with their ears.

In a few minutes my friend came out of the old Trading Post smiling; she had sold her beads. We drove off down the highway, part of the rushing traffic.

Yet for the remainder of that busy day there was a quiet joy in my heart.

Many times since that morning I have paused to remember that today with its joy or pain, blessing or sorrow, is mine now. God is with me today.

I have looked for the beauty of His works around me. Then my heart begins to swell in praise for the joy of awareness, the gladness of being alive and a part of His wonderful plan.

Yes, I have discovered the pause that really refreshes!

THE PERFECT PLACE

I know the perfect place to live. A place where the climate is better, the grass is greener, and the air is cleaner. A place where the people are friendly and the churches thriving.

Yes, I know a place where taxes are lower and unemployment almost unheard of. A place where you can get a good job and be appreciated.

I have heard of this place all of my life. I have met people of various races and creeds who speak wistfully of it.

I have even heard the announcer on our local radio station giving the weather report for this wonderful place. Nearly every day he will say: "It will be sunny and warmer (in the winter), or cooler (in the summer)"—Elsewhere!

Ah, that is the place to be: Elsewhere!

Who has not at one time or another longed to be there? We read of people in the Bible who yearned for Elsewhere. Remember Jonah? He was so sure Elsewhere was the answer to his problems that he bought a one-way ticket and tried to go there. Of course, he didn't quite make it. Seems there was a whale of a difference between Jonah's experiences and his dreams.

That seems to be a part of the problem. Things get in our way and hinder or stop us from running away to Elsewhere.

Do you ever wonder if someone is plotting to put roadblocks across your path? Roadblocks that keep you in the way of faithfulness and duty when you could be having so much fun Elsewhere?

Some people, however, manage to get around the roadblocks. With great determination they keep on the road to Elsewhere. A young man named Demas was one of those people.

Demas was really determined to do his own thing, and of course, Elsewhere, out there in the big exciting world, was the place to get it all together.

Paul, one man who evidently gave little thought to an earthly Elsewhere (his vision reached beyond this world) tells us about Demas. His remarks are brief, but they say a lot: "Demas hath forsaken me, having loved this present world" (2 Timothy 4:10).

The exact location of Elsewhere varies with our circumstances and our state of mind. It is not always "out there"; sometimes we may feel it is "back there."

For example: the children of Israel on the greatest adventure in history stiffened their necks and hardened their hearts and wailed to go back to Elsewhere—Egypt, in their case. This attitude brought judgment and death upon the nation. (See Numbers 11 and 14.) Quite a price to pay to indulge discontent!

Discontent? Yes, that is what lies at the root of the longing to be Elsewhere. Discontent—that feeling that we know what is best, and best is definitely not here.

Look into the Bible for the finest collection of case histories ever recorded. You will see that discontent stems from a lack of trust or faith and breeds rebellion and disobedience which, if not repented of, brings judgment and death. A dark picture.

Is there a remedy for discontent? Certainly! The Bible gives the prescription over and over. It is faith, trust in the Lord. If you want to read some brief case histories of people who used this prescription and found it to be 100 percent effective, read the 11th chapter of Hebrews.

Then Hebrews 12 starts out by speaking directly to us, whatever our situation might be. The writer urges us to lay aside every weight and every besetting sin and run our race with patience.

He says we can do this by "looking unto Jesus the author and

finisher of our faith; who for the joy that was set before him endured the cross, despising the shame, and is set down at the right
hand of the throne of God" (Hebrews 12:2).

So the next time discontent starts nibbling away your peace
and robbing you of your joy in Christ, read these chapters in Hebrews. Take the prescription of faith and apply it to your life.

You might also memorize some short verses for emergency
aid when you cannot get alone to read and meditate. Remember,
discontent is the opposite of content, and these verses speak of
the blessing of being content.

Perhaps you are discontented because you think you are not
getting ahead as quickly as you should. Or maybe you do not
have as many material possessions as you would like. If so, think
on this verse: "But godliness with contentment is great gain" (1
Timothy 6:6). Or, "And be content with such things as ye have: for
he hath said, I will never leave thee, nor forsake thee" (Hebrews
13:5).

Meditate on these verses. Praise the Lord that you are you and
that you are where you are.

If you ever need to be somewhere else, doing something else,
faith and praise will help you wait until He, the Lord, leads you
on. The Bible promises us that He will do this. So believe it; don't
fret over it.

Discontent and the longing for Elsewhere fades away as we apply faith and praise. Then we can say with Paul: "I have learned, in
whatsoever state [situation, place] I am, therewith to be content"
(Philippians 4:11).

THE SIGN OF THE SERPENT

The Sunday school teacher paused. He looked searchingly into the dark eyes of the Apache Indians that were fixed upon him as he earnestly expounded the Word of God in their language.

His gaze shifted; he looked toward the back of the church where the missionaries (my co-worker and I) were sitting.

We sat as members of his class because Apache Christians handle all our Sunday school program—from distributing lesson leaflets, ringing the early bell, taking care of the money, to teaching the seven classes.

That morning I sensed the teacher was about to break away from the lesson and speak directly to us.

I was right. With a slight smile and a sort of lifting of his head and pointing with the chin and lips toward us (the Indian way of pointing directions or indicating someone in particular), he said: "Sister Jo Ann, Sister Mamie, I want to say this in English so you will understand it all. I want to tell you what my father used to do."

He paused again, a faraway look on his gentle brown face. I could tell he was seeing with the eye of memory. Then in the soft voice that is typical of the Apache people he continued:

"I remember how we all lived up the canyon in wickiups." (A wickiup is a conical structure made of poles thatched with bear grass. It has a hole in the top through which the smoke of the small fire built on the dirt floor can escape.)

"We didn't know anything about Jesus, and it was a long, hard way to the hospital. So when the people got sick, they usually went first to the only one they knew of who could help them, a medicine man.

"My father was sort of a medicine man. But he never caused anything bad to happen to people, as some medicine men did; he only prayed for them to help them when they were sick.

"When he was going to pray for a sick person, first he would spread a blanket or a piece of canvas on the ground. On this he prepared what he needed for the ceremony. There was a reason for working on this blanket, for everything had to be kept together in one place. So when it was all over it could be taken out of the camp (the place where an Apache family lived) and put where no one would find it or bother it.

"My father would take a small piece of the center stalk of the bear grass plant and clean it, carefully scraping off all of the bark. Then he would carve it into the form of a snake. Using the ashes from the fire he made stripes on the carved snake; on the flattened end that was the head he made eyes from the ashes. When it was finished, he put the head end into the fire and let it start to burn.

"When it began to burn, he pulled it out of the fire and held it as he watched the flames die out. While the burned head was still very hot, he bit it off and chewed it up. Then he blew it on the sick person. He chanted many prayers while doing all this. Sometimes the sick person got better; it was all we knew to do.

But now we know about Jesus; He is our healer."

After telling this story the teacher finished the lesson in Apache. He aptly tied in this illustration which related so well to his fellow Apaches.

But I sat there deeply moved at the word picture he had painted for us. I could see it all vividly in my mind. The sick person, hurting, perhaps bewildered by pain. The blanket spread on the ground, the medicine man with the carved serpent in his hand, watchng it burn. I could almost hear the sputter of the dying flames.

Then another mental picture, just as vivid, filled my mind. I saw sick and dying people and a man also holding a carved serpent in his hand. But this serpent was carved from bronze. The man put it on a pole. All those who had been bitten by the living serpents among them had only to look on the bronze serpent hanging on the pole, and they lived (Numbers 21:9).

As I thought on this, I saw yet another picture. On a barren hill called Golgotha were three crosses. On the center cross writhed the tortured form of the One who had said: "And as Moses lifted up the serpent in the wilderness, even so must the Son of man be lifted up: that whosoever believeth in him should not perish, but have eternal life" (John 3: 14-15).

"Should not perish, but have eternal life." Thinking of those words, I felt joy like a rising tide flow into my heart. I remembered that the Sunday school teacher's father, the old medicine man who had done all he could to help his people with prayers to the serpent carved from a bear grass stalk, had only a few years before his death heard of the living Christ—the Christ who like the serpent in the wilderness was lifted up on the cross for all who would look, believe, and accept.

The old medicine man accepted Christ, and like the new Christians in Ephesus, upon his conversion he burned all his "curious arts" (Acts 19:19).

Now the old medicine man has passed through that doorway called death, but he did not perish. For by his faith in Jesus Christ he received eternal life.

Today his sons and grandson are leaders and teachers in the church. Thus the words of Jesus reach down through the centuries. They reach from ancient Jerusalem to a lowly wickiup in the remote mountains of Arizona. The words ring just as clear and true today as the day they were spoken: "And I, if I be lifted up from the earth, will draw all men unto me" (John 12:32).

UNFADING FLOWERS

When rain or snow comes to central and southern Arizona during the winter, a seeming magic bursts forth from the dry gray soil in the spring. Flowers scatter their brilliant hues across the hills and canyons. Lovely apricot shades of mallow, yellow marigolds, blue lupine, and many others paint the landscape with lavish beauty.

Especially profuse, and my favorite, are the gold poppies. These dainty little flowers cover the mesas, line the roadsides, and cascade over the canyon walls—a golden orange carpet of sunshine blowing joyfully in the spring breeze.

In a few short weeks the days will grow hotter, the winds will blow, and the poppies will vanish. By midsummer you would never know these hills were once clothed with beautiful flowers.

I looked at the poppies and remembered an allegory the Psalmist used to portray the brevity of life: "As for man, his days are like grass: as a flower of the field, so he flourisheth. For the wind passeth over it, and it is gone; and the place thereof shall know it no more" (Psalm 103: 15-16).

I have stood on a lonely hillside amid forgotten ruins. Once Indians lived here. Their lives bloomed like the golden poppies.

Now they are gone. Only a few pieces of broken pottery and crumbling walls testify of their former existence.

I have stood looking into sunken graves. According to the dates crudely cut on rough rocks, they are from the early 1920's.

I could see the cedar limbs used first to lay the body on and then to cover the body—no white man's casket in those days.

Who were they? Just some Indians who once flourished like the flowers on these hills. But the wind of time passed over, and they are gone. Few even recall where their graves are.

I stood by an open grave on a gray December day, the sky threatening snow. We had come to lay to rest one whose life had bloomed for many years on these desolate hills.

We traveled miles to this lonely place. At first glance I thought no one else was buried here, but eventually I could detect rough mounds and the hand-carved dates on rocks here and there.

I remembered the first time I met the dear old lady we had come here to bury. She was living then in a wickiup, the conical grass-thatched shelter which until recently served as the typical home of the Apaches.

A group of Christian Apache women from the Cibecue church, where I was then working, felt led of the Lord to visit this old lady, Helena Henry.

We drove up and down and over a rough dusty road that I thought would never end. Finally we reached a camp—a group of three or four wickiups. I timidly followed the Indian ladies into the camp.

They conversed briefly in Apache with a woman who had stepped out to meet us. Then motioning me to follow, they went into the largest wickiup.

As my eyes adjusted to the dim light, I saw an old woman lying on a cot. Her eyes were bright, her breathing labored. Even on this warm day she was covered with a blanket.

The women began talking to her. Although I couldn't understand, I knew they were telling her about Jesus. After a while they said to me, "She wants prayer and she will believe in Jesus." We prayed, her voice joining ours, tears streaming down her wrinkled brown cheeks.

When we had finished praying, the ladies talked to her again at great length. But before we left, she told me, as the ladies interpreted: "I feel better now and I believe in Jesus. I'll come to the church if you'll come after me."

We went after her, and she did come to nearly every service. Not long after that I left Cibecue. I had been here in Carrizo several years when someone told me that an old lady from Cibecue had moved here to live near her son. "She is a Christian," they said, "and she wants to come to church."

I went to visit her and at once recognized Helena Henry. For nearly 2 years she faithfully attended the church. Then her health failed, and in December she went to be with Jesus.

Standing by her grave I thought that this too was a life that had flourished like the flowers of the field. And over it that wind of time had passed. But there was a tremendous difference between this life and some of the other Indians, for this life continued to blossom!

For she was "born again, not of corruptible seed, but of incor-

ruptible, by the Word of God, which liveth and abideth for ever"
(1 Peter 1:23).

Those who are truly born of God are unfading flowers, for they
have eternal life.

As Jesus said: "I am the resurrection and the life: he that believeth in me, though he were dead, yet shall he live. And whosoever liveth and believeth in me shall never die" (John 11:25-26).

We committed the body of our dear sister to the ground to
await the resurrection—knowing that already, as an unfading
flower, she was enjoying eternal life in God's garden above.

WAKE IN APACHE LAND

When someone dies it is the
custom of the White Mountain
Apaches to have a wake, which
usually lasts for two days and
nights. Relatives and friends
gather from across the reservation for this social function of
great importance. They help by
bringing groceries and assisting
with the cooking, serving and
tending of fires. In addition to
the daily meals they also serve
a large meal at midnight each
night.

The tribal organization sup-
plies rough lumber to build
windbreaks, which usually have
three sides. There may be three
or four of them opening into
each other. These windbreaks
are floorless, roofless enclosures, with rough benches running

along the inside walls, and are large enough for thirty or forty
people. At least one large fire is burning in the center of each
windbreak. In cold weather the Indians carry shovelfuls of hot
coals from the large fire and place them at intervals in front of
the people huddled on the benches. Sometimes they build several other small fires for additional warmth.

They use one of the enclosures for cooking. Great pots of
beans simmer over the coals, five gallon cans of coffee steam
beside the fires, and meat is roasting or boiling. Women in bright-
colored camp dresses with full skirts trimmed with rickrack sit,
usually on the ground, making dozens of large tortillas. Some of
the women will be bending over the fire minding skillets of siz-
zling fry bread. The pungent odor of burning wood permeates
everything. Ashes flutter through the air settling in the coffee,
the food, and your hair, but no one seems to mind.

If the dead person was a Christian or has close relatives who
are Christians, probably a phonograph will be playing gospel
music (if electricity is available) near where the body is lying in
one of the larger buildings. If the wake is being held at one of
the new homes, built under the Government Self Help Housing
Program, the casket may be on the back porch. The yard will be
walled in with the rough boards and divided into the several
rooms.

In the past years after caskets came into use on the reservation
the tribe provided the casket. In some cases the tribe still helps
pay for it, and they always send men from the jail to dig the grave.
If a funeral director is not in charge, and only in the last few
years has there been a funeral director to call on, the missionary
helps the family make the necessary arrangements. There was no
funeral director present for the first three funerals I conducted
on the reservation.

A beautiful Pendleton blanket is often draped over half of the
casket. There will be many plastic flowers and some lovely handmade crepe paper flowers. Bright-colored crepe paper streamers

always decorate the area where the open casket is situated. If the deceased was a man, a new western hat will be lying on his folded hands.

A great deal of drinking may occur during the wake, but many of the Apache people do riot approve of this. Some try to keep alcoholic drinks from being brought into the area where the wake is being held. It is also customary to invite the various churches of the community to come and conduct a service at the wake. Since we have the only church in this small community, we have a service each night during every wake. This is a wonderful opportunity to present the gospel, especially to some who would never enter a church.

The Christian Indians sing a number of songs; then one by one they testify to the saving, delivering power of Jesus. Next, the missionary is expected to preach, and there is no time limit. Many of the people will stay there all night anyway.

Many are the wake services I have attended, standing beside a roaring fire with one side of me slowly roasting, the other freezing. I have stood under the sparkling stars, the wood ashes sifting silently over me. With my heart full of joy I have listened to the Apache Christians sing "Amazing Grace." Sometimes they sing in Apache, and the words to that old song so loved by the Indians, "There'll Be No Dark Valleys When Jesus Comes," are hauntingly beautiful sung in the Apache language.

The songs go drifting out into the night —into the hearts of Apaches who are listening within the walled-in enclosures or standing around the huge fires built on the outside. People on the outside may be laughing and talking loudly; some may be drinking or quarreling. Soon, however, the noise dies and you know folk are listening—hungry hearts who walk in darkness, seeking vainly through the medicine man, through their ancient ways, to find light; hearts that are weary, hurt, frustrated. Many have turned to alcohol to try to escape the darkness and the problems of life.

So, in the midst of death at the wake, we proclaim the good news of the gospel that brings life and light. The seed is planted; another may water it with testimony or perhaps tears. Then, the Lord of the harvest will give the increase. He will draw seeking hearts to Himself.

When the students from the American Indian Bible Institute in Phoenix, Arizona, sing the song, "There'll Be No Dark Valleys," they sing it "No More Reservations When Jesus Comes." How true, for Jesus said, "Many shall come from the east and west, and shall sit down (together)… in the kingdom of heaven." Indians from every tribe will be there, perhaps some who heard the good news for the first time at a wake.

'WHAT IS HIS NAME?'

Morning on the desert! The air so clear the jagged gray-blue peaks of the far mountains look almost close enough to reach out and touch. It is quiet, even beyond quietness; there is a pristine stillness and freshness in this strange and lovely land! Even the sheep seem to sense it. In recognition of the superb beauty, their incessant baaing is subdued.

The man, gaunt and browned by the desert sun, leans heavily on his staff. His piercing dark eyes scan the rugged landscape, alert to every detail. He too senses something different—some expectation in the bright clear air.

Then, without warning, the silence is shattered by the hiss and crackle of fire. A small bush suddenly has burst into flames. As the man turns aside to watch, he is amazed—not at the fire. He has seen burning bushes on this desert before. Rather his sense of wonder is aroused—and he goes to investigate—because the bush, though engulfed in flames, remains whole!

What happened when Moses, that man on the desert—tending his father-in-law's sheep—turned aside to see a bush that burned but was not consumed is a matter of history. It will be remembered that Moses on that long-ago day had a question for God. He asked: "When I come unto the children of Israel, and shall say unto them, the God of your fathers hath sent me unto you; and they shall say to me, What is his name? What shall I say unto them?" (Exodus 3:13).

What is His name?

The Apache woman stood with bowed head beside the charred remains and smoking ashes—all that was left of her wickiup. Gone! Everything gone: the saddle, the blankets, the corn.

Only the horses were left, and at least one of them would be given to the medicine man to pay for the ceremony needed—a ceremony to try to determine the cause of the fire and to protect from further disasters. If someone were working witchcraft, or if for unknown reasons the spirits were offended, protection would be needed; and it wouldn't come cheaply.

Bessie, that Apache woman, sighed deeply as she turned to help her husband Sam poke through the rubble with a stick, looking for anything they could use. The few things they found they were afraid to take lest part of the curse might be on those items.

Hurriedly husband and wife put their two small children on the horses with them—the baby in a cradle board was on Bessie's back. Without a backward glance they rode away. They would find another place for a camp, and Bessie would build another wickiup.

Huddled near the fire that night Bessie tried to sleep, but she couldn't forget the sight of the smoking ruins of all they once had owned. Why? Why? Wasn't there anyone, any strong spirit, any god who could love them and protect them? With all her heart she wished, if there were such, she knew about him.

The days passed. The new wickiup was built, and relatives shared blankets and corn. Bessie, however, could not get away from memories of the loss of the first wickiup. She continued to wonder if a god existed who loved and helped people. If such a god existed, repeatedly she asked herself, What is His name? The Indian woman told no one of her thoughts and desires.

One night Bessie had a dream. In the dream she did not see anyone, but she heard a man talking in her language (in Apache).

"Someday," she heard, "a man will come and tell you about the God who loves people."

Upon awakening the following morning Bessie had an unusual peace in her heart and an expectancy. She decided to tell no person of the dream; she would wait for the man to come—the man who would tell her about the God who loves people. Following that, she no longer would have to wonder about His name.

Years passed. The children grew to adulthood. Still Bessie waited. Then in 1957, she heard news of a white man and his wife coming to their village, Carrizo. The white man, Bessie learned, was telling people about the God who loved them.

She knew that stranger must be the man in her dream. Only

then did she tell her husband about the dream of so long ago, details of which still were vivid to her.

Thus it was in July 1957, that Bessie and Sam made their way to a service Missionary-pastor Elmer Kaufmann and his wife Edna were holding under a brush arbor in Carrizo.* Bessie and Sam could not understand English, but some Christian Apache women explained the gospel to them. At the close of the service Bessie and Sam made their way together to the front.

"We want to take the Jesus way," Sam said.

At last Bessie had come to know His name. She found the joy and peace only He can give for she was saved; furthermore, she understood what it meant to be saved.

Not long after taking the "Jesus way" Sam became quite ill. Pastor Kaufmann visited Sam and Bessie in their wickiup one evening. As the minister knelt on the dirt floor by Sam, he realized Sam was dying. The missionary, his arms around Sam, prayed, "Lord, receive his spirit." Sam went home to be with Jesus.

In the years following Sam's death Bessie learned, as did Moses, that the great "I Am," the ever-present God, who loved her, has many names. Some of those names, she knew, were "Wonderful, Counselor, The mighty God, The everlasting Father, The Prince of Peace." But Bessie just called Him "Jesus." Without once turning back, she continued to walk in the "Jesus way."

When Bessie died in January 1984, her obituary said she was nearly 100. People in her village thought she was a little past 100.

Bessie saw many changes come to her people. She herself experienced some changes. Those who knew her are confident she would say the best thing that ever happened in her extended life span was coming to know His name. To her it brought that essential transformation indicated in the message of the angel to Mary so long ago: "Thou shalt call his name Jesus: for he shall save his people from their sins" (Matthew 1:21).

WHEN IT SEEMS LIKE CHRISTMAS

It just doesn't seem like Christmas. Have you ever felt that way? Said that? I have, for Christmas is not just a date on the calendar, it is a state of mind!

When the Christmas season comes, we expect to feel differently. Perhaps we are longing for that warm glow within that comes from being loved, from belonging. That inward glow which was so much a part of childhood, of Christmas past.

When Christmas was the high-point of the whole year, we anticipated it for many excitement-filled weeks. Just as the snow we usually had where I grew up clothed the earth in radiant white beauty, even so Christmas seemed to cover the harshness of life with love, understanding, and joy. Yes, it always seemed like Christmas then.

But the years come, bringing with them the duties, burdens, cares of life—call them what you will. If we are not careful, they have a way of dulling our dreams, of taking the sparkle out of the soul.

The time comes when we realize that Christmas is almost upon us—again. But it just doesn't seem like Christmas. Oh yes, there are programs to be planned, cards waiting to be mailed, cooking, shipping, cleaning—all clamoring to be done. But what has happened to the joy, the lifted heart, the feeling of Christmas?

Do you know what I mean? Have you ever felt like the "oil of gladness" was at such a low ebb in your soul it was allowing the friction of life to cause sparks of doubt?

My coworker and I were nearing the edge of this slough of despond shortly before Christmas last year. As home missionaries, we are totally involved in our ministry among the White Mountain Apache Indians.

We were knee-deep in the external things of Christmas. Stacks of mail awaited an answering card from us. Quilts and gifts needed to be sorted and wrapped. We had Sunday school treats to prepare, decorations to put up, and program practice to look after. On and on, no end of work; but with it all, it just didn't seem like Christmas.

One day as we were lamenting how unlike Christmas it felt, we were interrupted by loud, urgent knocking at our front door. We both rushed to open the door. Two boys (about 8 and 10 years old), brothers who live near us, were standing on our porch.

Though it was not bitterly cold that day, the December wind was sharp, and I felt its chill as I stood in the open door. The boys wore no coats; their shirts and faded jeans had seen better days, and one was barefoot.

We knew these boys well and knew their mother could have done more for them. But the poor woman, deserted by her husband and left with a large family to raise alone, had turned to drink to escape her problems. We had tried to help her find security in Christ and were still praying for her.

But here stood two of her boys, as they had stood often before at our door, sometimes in tears, sometimes hungry. Only today they were smiling, the light of happiness shining in their bright eyes.

"Come in," we said, opening wide the door.

"We brought ya somethin'," they chorused as they bounced into the house. "Yeah, a Christmas present. We fixed it ourself," one remarked as they proudly handed each of us a small package.

We took the gifts which were wrapped carefully in wrinkled paper that had obviously wrapped other presents. One was tied with a soiled shoestring; the other was held together with a piece of twisted wire.

"Now put 'em under your tree," they suggested.

"Of course we will, and thank you," we both replied.

"Oh, it ain't much," explained the older boy, suddenly shy, digging his toes into the rug and pushing far down into his pockets. "But you know them people from Phoenix gave everybody a treat."

I remembered that a group of Army Reserves had visited our community a few days before and passed out hard candy, oranges, and small toys.

Knowing what a treat indeed the candy and oranges were to these boys, I felt a lump in my throat, and tears burned my eyes as I desperately blinked them away. For I suddenly realized as I gripped the small package that I was holding part of that treat— two oranges and some hard candy.

"We got to go now; we just wanted to give you somethin'," the older boy said as they went out the door, still smiling. On the porch they looked back and called out,

"Merry Christmas."

"Merry Christmas to you too, and thank you, thank you very much," we answered.

We put the presents under our little tree and were quiet for a long time. The words, "We just wanted to give ya somethin'," kept ringing in my ears.

That's really what makes Christmas giving something and accepting what's given. I realized I had been looking for meaning, for joy, in the material things associated with Christmas, losing sight of the fact that God, our loving Father, had just wanted to give us something.

John 3:16 explains this: "For God so loved the world, that he gave his only begotten Son, that whosoever believeth in him should not perish, but have everlasting life. - And 2 Corinthians 9:15 should be our response to His love offering: "Thanks be unto God for his unspeakable gift."

Before long I was humming a Christmas carol. My cup of joy was full—and it really seemed like Christmas.